Contemplation
Before Sleep

Contemplation Before Sleep

B⬚XTREE

A Rebel Book

Second edition. All rights reserved.

First published in Great Britain in 1995 by Boxtree Limited

Copyright © Osho International 1991

The right of Osho International to be identified as Author of this Work
has been asserted by them in accordance with the Copyright, Designs
and Patents Act 1988

1 3 5 7 9 10 8 6 4 2

Designed by Blackjacks
Compiled by Jivan Mary Amoore QSM
Cover design by Ma Deva Sandipa

Printed and Bound in Great Britain by
Cox & Wyman, Reading, Berkshire

A CIP catalogue entry for this book is available from the British Library

ISBN: 1 7522 1671 6

"I don't teach you any dogma, any belief system, any philosophy. I simply give you the science of going in, of waking up your soul."

Osho

INTRODUCTION

To be used by itself or in conjunction with *Morning Contemplation*, this volume of passages excerpted from the talks of an enlightened master, Osho, with his disciples and other seekers, can provide the perfect way to end the day.

It is said that the last thought in one's mind as one falls asleep is also the first thought on waking. Perhaps the majority of us fall asleep with minds crammed with images from a television drama, with worries about the day that has passed and anxieties about the day that is to follow. A good many of us have trouble entering sleep at all.

The pieces selected have been specially chosen for the night-time. The quotations used in the morning contemplation book are stimulating, sometimes pithy, sometimes exuberant – always endorsing a lively, total participation in the day to come. By contrast, Osho's words in this evening volume will remind the reader of the significance of relaxation, expansion, melting, letting go.

"Month one" need not necessarily be the beginning of the calendar year but is the first month that you begin reading. The passages have been designed to be read consecutively rather than randomly, as Osho's understanding of life is revealed day by day. The pieces for the evening also make a continuum with the morning extract.

CONTEMPLATION BEFORE SLEEP

There is a particular way to use this book. It is not intended to be read as a novel but one passage at a time. It is to provide the reader not with a full meal to digest but with an after-dinner mint to round off the day. Osho's words are spoken not to induce agreement or disagreement, discussion or analysis. Osho has even said that it is not necessary to remember his words.

"If what I am saying to you is becoming a reality in your life, who cares whether you remember my words or not? It is perfectly right not to remember them; any remembrance of the words will be an obstruction. Let only pure meaning spread to the deepest core of your being where words have no access, where only wordless meaning is able to enter."

In fact, reading his words is more like listening to music than doing any mental exercise. Listening to music – or wine-tasting: take a sip, smell the bouquet and allow the flavour to tickle your spiritual palate.

Ma Prem Maneesha
Poona, India

MONTH 1

Be a Columbus of consciousness

The world is suffering too much because for the first time in the history of human consciousness, man has lost track of existence. Nobody has ever suffered like us. People have been poor in the past, very poor; people have starved, but people have never been spiritually so poor. People have never starved spiritually so much as today. My whole work is to give you back an insight into existence. Unless man becomes rooted in existence again man has no future.

CONTEMPLATION BEFORE SLEEP

Man has the potential of becoming a song of love, a dance of love, but very few people, very rare people, transform their potential into the actual. They are born as seeds, almost all die as seeds; their life remains nothing but a long experiment in futility.

My observation is that people go to the temples and the synagogues and the churches only out of fear, not out of love. Yes, older people go more often because they have become more afraid of death. They don't go to the church or the temple because they have known something tremendously valuable in life, but because life is slipping out of their hands and the great darkness of death is coming closer and they are afraid. They want someone to protect them.

Now they know that their money is not going to be with them, their friends are not going to be with them, their families will leave them. Out of desperation they start clinging to the idea of a God. But this is not out of love and this is not out of gratitude. And a God born out of fear is a false God.

My whole effort here is to make windows into existence available so that you don't go to God out of fear, so that you can go through the experience of beauty, through the experience of creativity, through the experience of love. And when a person goes through these experiences, the contact is tremendous, transforming. A single living contact with existence is enough – you will never be the same again.

day **3**

It is only with great challenges that one becomes integrated, that one's life energies become crystallized. Remember that. Never associate religion with fear; associate it with fearlessness, with courage, with such a courage that can help you go into the uncharted.

It is like going into the rough ocean in a small boat without any map, not knowing anything about the other shore. It is going like Columbus – just purely on the assumption that the earth is round, with the hope that one will reach somewhere. One has to be a Columbus of consciousness.

CONTEMPLATION BEFORE SLEEP

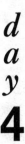
My suggestion is: start searching for love, not for a God directly, because if you search for a God directly, your God will be just your imagination. It will be a Hindu God, or a Mohammedan God or a Christian God...it will not be a true God.

Seek via love, because one thing is beautiful about love which is not so with a God: love is neither Christian, nor Hindu, nor Mohammedan.... Love is simply love without any adjective to it.

That is something tremendously beautiful about love. If humanity starts searching for love instead of a God, we can easily create a great brotherhood of humanity.

d
a
y

5

The moment you say 'God', it seems a very faraway thing. That's what they have been saying down the centuries, that God is somewhere above – in the sky very very far away. But when you say 'love', it is very close to the heart.

All those priests are cunning and crafty. They have been trying to prove that God is far away, because if God is far away, only then can they be the representatives of God, the mediators, the agents.

The moment you use the word 'God', it gives you a sense of person. God becomes limited, becomes defined. But love is not a person, it is a quality, a presence, a fragrance, not a flower – more unlimited, more unbounded, more infinite. When you say 'God', you simply feel impotent – "What to do?" But if love is there you can do something about it. It is your innermost nature to be loving; hence my whole teaching revolves around the word 'love'.

Jesus says, "God is love."

I say, "Love is God."

CONTEMPLATION BEFORE SLEEP

A man of love knows how to live wholly because he lives totally. His body is full of love; his body cells are dancing in love; his mind is full of love – not full of logic, but full of love. His heart is full of love – it is not just a blood-purifying system, not just a breathing instrument; he breathes love in, and breathes love out. His very soul is nothing but pure love, an ocean of love.

Such a person is bound to find existence. Where can existence hide from such a person? And in fact such a person need not go in search of existence, existence comes in search of him. And that is the beauty: when existence comes seeking and searching for you.

d
a
y

7

L ove unreservedly.
Love the whole existence. It is one reality. The trees and the mountains and the people are not really different. We all participate together, we exist in a deep harmony. We go on breathing in oxygen, and breathing out carbon dioxide. Trees go on breathing in carbon dioxide, and breathing out oxygen. Now, without trees we will not be able to exist. We are joined together, we interpenetrate. And that's how the whole existence is interlinked.

So love unreservedly – the trees, the stars, the mountains, the people, the animals. The point is not to whom you are loving, the point is that you are loving.

CONTEMPLATION BEFORE SLEEP

Man's well-being is with existence. If we become rooted in existence, we are whole and healthy. If we remain without existence, we remain without roots, without nourishment.

Existence is the earth, our nourishment, our well-being. And the whole of life is nothing but an exploration – an exploration of the source of our well-being.

MONTH ONE

d
a
y
9

Existence can be contacted only in total surrender. Less than that won't do. Just as water evaporates at one hundred degrees, it is total surrender when the ego evaporates, when you are just an empty space. Nobody is inside. There is a great silence, infinite, unbounded, but nobody is there.

That is the moment when the whole sky descends in you, when the earth and the sky meet, when you are transformed from a mortal being into an immortal soul.

CONTEMPLATION BEFORE SLEEP

Man has to go beyond his will so that he can become part of the divine will. One has to drop one's own will; it is the whole trouble. Once our will is dissolved, then existence starts functioning through us. Then there is no misery, no anxiety. One is utterly relaxed; there is no problem.

All problems arise out of your will, because will means fighting with the whole. It is struggle, and struggle is bound to bring tension. And you are doomed to fail; hence, however hard one fights, one knows deep down in the heart, deep down somewhere that it is futile, one cannot succeed against the whole.

One can succeed only with the whole, not against the whole. And the moment you surrender your will, all is yours. Suddenly the whole universe opens its doors for you. All the mysteries become available to you, all the secrets are handed over to you, all the keys. The paradox is, in surrendering the will, you become the master. And in keeping the will and fighting for it, you will remain a slave.

d
a
y
11

People are hard. Life prepares them to be hard because life prepares them to fight. Slowly slowly, they lose all inner softness; they become rocklike. And a rocklike person is a dead person. He lives only in name, he does not truly live.

True life consists of softness, vulnerability, openness. Don't be afraid of existence: existence cares for you, loves you. There is no need to fight with existence. Existence is ready to give more than you can ever ask for or you can ever imagine. But existence can give only if you are soft, vulnerable. If you are porous then it can enter from everywhere.

Be porous, be available to existence, unafraid. There is no need to be afraid. It is our existence, we belong to it; it belongs to us.

CONTEMPLATION BEFORE SLEEP

Religion has to be real now. Enough is enough. We have lived with the unreal long enough. Life is real and love is real, and when you are in love with life, life becomes your whole existence. And the only way to worship life is to sing, to dance, to bloom, to be creative; to contribute something to the celebration, to contribute something to this great festival, this great carnival that goes on and on! The stars are dancing, and the trees are dancing and the oceans are dancing.

My sannyasins have to become part of the oceans, and the trees, and the clouds, and the stars. This is my temple – I don't trust in any other temple, I don't believe in any God. This is my experience and I want to share it with my people.

To be a sannyasin simply means that now you are moving into the festive dimension. It is an invitation to the spring, it is getting ready for the spring.

d
a
y

13

Friedrich Nietzsche says: "God is dead."
But nobody has asked him, "Who killed him?"
There are only two possibilities: either he committed
suicide or he was murdered. And God cannot commit
suicide; that is impossible, because God means bliss.
Why should bliss commit suicide? God means truth.
Why would truth commit suicide? God really means
eternity; hence suicide is impossible. He must have
been killed.

The priests have done it. All the priests of all the
religions have been part of the great conspiracy; they
have killed God. Of course they cannot kill the real
God, but they can kill the God that they themselves
created. Because of ten thousand years of stupid
history in the name of religion, I suggest: seek love,
forget all about God. And godliness is going to come
of its own accord. It is bound to come, it is inevitable.

CONTEMPLATION BEFORE SLEEP

The body is born and the body dies; the mind is born and the mind dies. But you are neither the body nor the mind.

You are something transcendental to both, something which never dies and which is never born. You have always been here and will always be here.

The moment one starts feeling it, the whole perspective on life starts changing. Whatsoever has been important up to that moment becomes unimportant: money, power, prestige and all that.

And whatsoever has never been important before suddenly gains great importance: love, compassion, meditation, prayer, godliness.

Remember that within you there is something which is eternal.

d
a
y

15

Jesus says that the kingdom of God is within you. That is the essential teaching of all the awakened ones: don't go anywhere; don't seek and search outside yourself, you will not find anything there. You will remain empty, unfulfilled, frustrated, because the real kingdom, the real riches are part of your interiority, of your subjectivity, of your soul.

Ordinary humanity is extrovert. If you move in exactly the opposite direction it is introversion. Not that I am against the world, but not to know oneself is very dangerous. Once you know yourself you can roam all over the world sharing your joy and living your joy; then there is no problem. If you are rooted in your being you can be as extrovert as you want, nothing can harm you. You can live in the market-place, but your meditation will remain undisturbed.

But the first, the foremost thing is to settle within, to be acquainted with your inner reality. And my whole effort is to turn you inwards, in every possible way, to help you to go inwards.

I cannot give you the truth, nobody can, but I can indicate where it is to be found. It is not to be found on the moon, it is not to be found on Everest; it is to be found just within you.

Learn to close your eyes and see within.

CONTEMPLATION BEFORE SLEEP

All is divine. In fact there is no God, only godliness. God is not a person but a quality, not a person but a presence.

The idea of God as a person is anthropomorphic: we have made that image in our own image. It is nothing but man projected; it is not the true God. That's why Buddha is silent about God; he talks about godliness but never about God.

My own experience is exactly the same: there is no God but there is godliness; the whole existence is overflowing with godliness. There is no division between God and the world; existence is divine.

Start looking at existence with this vision, with these eyes, and you will be surprised because you will start seeing things you had never seen before. You have been passing the same things every day: the same trees and the same birds and the same people. But once you have this vision that all is divine, you start looking at things in a new light. Then the world is no more a puzzle, no more a problem, no more a question – not a question to be solved but a mystery to be lived.

day

17

Godliness is our substance, our very being. It is not something outside us, it is our innermost core, our interiority. We are not to seek and search for it. This has only to be remembered: we have forgotten it. Our godliness is not lost, it is only that we have forgotten who we are.

M an is capable of becoming a host to existence, a home to existence. And unless one becomes a host and a home to existence, one remains unfulfilled. Without allowing existence in, one remains in a deep frustration, because the moment existence enters into our being, we become existence. That is our ultimate destiny. Only with its fulfilment is there contentment and the joy of arriving.

d
a
y
18

d
a
y
19

We are very close to existence, but like parallel lines we go on, never meeting. Once we stop going into the past and the future, the parallel lines start coming closer and closer together. One day, suddenly, there is only one line: The two lines have merged. That is the moment of great joy, great benediction. That's what everyone is seeking, longing for. And because people go on missing it, they become miserable.

Be ready. And the only way to be ready is to live in the present, and you will become a home for existence. That is the fulfilment of life.

CONTEMPLATION BEFORE SLEEP

Existence is our only security. Money, power, prestige – nothing is secure. Family, friends, even life itself – nothing is secure. We are surrounded by insecurity.

There is one thing which is secure, and that one thing cannot be found anywhere outside. That one thing can only be found at the innermost core. God resides there. That is God's dwelling place – the heart of your hearts!

And to know the God within is to go beyond all security. Then everything is safe and secure. And when everything is safe and secure, misery disappears naturally, anxiety disappears, and great bliss arises. That bliss is the deepest longing of your being.

d
a
y
21

The victory is through knowing the secret. And there is only one secret worth knowing, that is your own innermost self. That is the secretmost place.

People go on travelling far and wide; that is not difficult. Man has reached the moon – it is so easy. But it is very difficult to reach one's own centre, and the secret of the secrets is hidden there, the master key which can unlock all the mysteries.

By being a sannyasin you are entering the path of self-discovery. It is already there, we have only to discover it. Just a few unnecessary things have to be removed, a few curtains, and suddenly we are face to face with God himself. The secret is that we are gods, and the misery is that we have become beggars.

CONTEMPLATION BEFORE SLEEP

The first thing to remember is that life has been given to us, it is not our achievement. In fact we don't deserve it at all. It is a very strange law of existence that those who deserve it – a Buddha, a Christ – disappear from life, and those who don't deserve it, go on getting life again and again. Once you deserve it you are ready to disappear into the ultimate. If you don't deserve it you will have to come back.

And the second thing to remember is strength of the spirit. It is not something that is yours either, it is God's constant flowing in you. You are breathing Him every moment, unconsciously of course. The moment you become conscious, you will be surprised. We eat God, we breathe God – there is nothing else but God. He is our nourishment. He is our roots, he is our branches, the foliage, the flowers, the fruit. He is all and we are nothing.

d
a
y
23

The most difficult thing in life is to receive a gift, because it goes against the ego. It is easier to give, very easy to give. But to receive is very difficult. And to receive when you don't deserve – then it becomes even more difficult. And we don't deserve – we have not earned it. We are not worthy of bliss, but existence goes on giving; not because we deserve, but because it has it in such abundance. The moment you receive its bliss, it feels thankful to you. You have unburdened it, you have taken a little weight from its being. But remember, it is very difficult to receive a gift. It feels like a humiliation. One feels a little embarrassed. A sannyasin has to learn how to receive a gift in great joy and celebration, because the more you become receptive, the more will be given to you. If you are totally receptive the whole of heaven can descend into your being this very moment, here and now. All that is needed on your part is to be absolutely open and ready.

CONTEMPLATION BEFORE SLEEP

All the masters of all the ages have declared that everybody is born a divine king but is utterly unaware of the fact. Not knowing our own inner world, we remain unaware of our kingdom. And because we are unaware of the kingdom that belongs to us, that is forever ours, we go on desiring small things, begging for small things.

We are dreaming that we are beggars. The moment one wakes up, one is in for a great surprise: one finds one is not a beggar, one is a king.

That's the whole purpose of meditation – to make you aware of your kingdom, to make you aware of your highest potential. And once you start becoming aware, then the journey is not difficult. Just a little awakening and then the sleep is almost gone, then things become easier. But unless you are awake, it cannot be a reality, it cannot be a realization.

d
a
y

25

Once you are aware you start seeking and searching for a second birth. And the second birth becomes possible only through meditation. The first birth is through the mother, the second birth is through meditation; hence, in ancient scriptures, meditation is called the real mother.

Jesus says to his disciples, "Unless you are born again you will not enter into the kingdom of God." In the East, the person who has attained to God is called *dwij*, twice born. The second birth releases the fragrance.

CONTEMPLATION BEFORE SLEEP

The Western meditation is nothing but a kind of thinking. Thinking of higher things is called meditation. When you think of God, when you think of Christ, when you think of love, it is called meditation.

In the East, thinking is not meditation at all. Whether you think of God or of money doesn't matter; any thinking of any object is a disturbance in meditation. In the East, meditation means a state of no thought, just pure being. And that is the greatest experience in life – when you simply exist. No thought crosses your being, the whole traffic stops, the mind disappears. But consciousness is there and more than ever, because whatsoever was hidden behind the thoughts is no longer hidden. Whatsoever was involved in thoughts is no longer involved. All energy is released. One is simply a pool of energy, and so silent that not even a ripple arises.

In that silent pool of consciousness, of energy, existence is reflected; we come to know that which is. God is another name for 'that which is'.

d
a
y
27

The only preparation required to experience godliness is to put the mind aside. That's what meditation is all about – a strategy to stop this constantly chattering mind, this crazy mind that goes on and on for no reason at all. It is busy without any business.

I am not saying that the mind has to be destroyed; it has only to be put aside so when you need it you can use it. It is like your car parked in the garage. When you want to use it you can take it out of the garage, then you are the master.

But ordinarily, the situation has become just the reverse: the car insists on not going into the garage. The car says, "I am not going to stop." The car says, "You have to run with me." And it goes on running, twenty-four hours a day. Even while you are asleep the mind goes on and on. Ordinarily once it starts in childhood it never stops before death, unless somebody starts moving into meditation.

For the very few who enter into meditation mind stops, suddenly they become aware of the sun that was hiding behind the clouds of the mind. That awareness of the ultimate light, of the ultimate sun, is divine knowledge.

CONTEMPLATION BEFORE SLEEP

We go on listening to the outside, hence we go on missing the inner voice. It speaks from your innermost core. We live on the periphery, we live in the mind, and the mind is so noisy that it does not allow us to hear the still, small voice within. A master is needed only as a device, because you hear the outside. The master says from the outside what existence has been trying to tell you from the inside for centuries.

Being with the master is simply getting ready to turn inwards one day, so that you can close your eyes and look in, so that you can start hearing what your own intuition goes on telling you. And the intuition is always right. The intellect may be right, may be wrong, it is always either/or; doubt persists, it is never indubitable. But intuition is without any doubt, it simply knows. The intuitive person never repents because he never does anything wrong, he cannot. He simply follows the voice of existence within.

d
a
y
29

You are not the body, nor the mind either; you are the witness of it all. Unless one grows more and more in witnessing, one will not know that one is a soul.

You become aware of your eyes only when you see. If you keep your eyes closed, you will forget all about them. If a child is never allowed to use his legs he will not be able to walk and he will forget all about his legs.

It is by using a certain faculty that we become aware of it. By seeing we become aware that we have eyes, by hearing we become aware that we have ears, by smelling we become aware that we have a nose. Exactly like that, by witnessing one becomes aware that one has a soul. Witnessing is the function of the soul.

That has been the search in the East: how to become a witness of all, just a watcher, a pure watcher with no identification. You are just looking at the body and the mind and all their functions and their activities and movements, but you are simply a watcher standing by the side of the road – the traffic goes on. You are neither the car moving, nor the truck, nor the bus, nor the people, nor the buffaloes nor the cows – nobody. You are simply the watcher standing by the side of the road.

That's what meditation is: to see your body-mind complex without becoming identified with it. And soon a totally new phenomenon is experienced: the existence of the soul. That's my whole work here: to make you aware that you are gods and goddesses, that you are eternal beings.

CONTEMPLATION BEFORE SLEEP

What is courage? The most significant definition is the capacity to drop the familiar, the known, because that's what mind is – the familiar, the known, the past. And the moment you drop the past, you open up to infinities. But man is afraid to be so open, man feels lost in that vast space.

Mind is a small thing. It feels cosy, warm. It is like a golden cage. It is beautiful, you can decorate it – and everybody tries to decorate it. That's what our education is for: to decorate the golden cage and make it so beautiful that it becomes almost impossible for you to leave it. You start clinging to it. You forget that you have wings, that the whole sky is a challenge, that you have to go to the stars, that there is a long, long journey ahead.

Hence my definition of courage is the capacity to drop the golden cage of the mind and to go into the unknown, in spite of all the fears, in spite of the insecurity of it all. Only the person who has that quality is religious.

Life is synonymous with God. God is not the creator of life, but life itself; he is not separate from life. The very idea of the creator is false. He is not like a painter, because the painter becomes separate from the painting. He is more like a dancer; he remains one with it.

Hence, to worship God one need not go to a temple, to a mosque, to a synagogue. Life is more than is needed. This whole earth, this whole existence, is full of God, overflowing with God. He is the green and the red and the gold of the trees. He is all over the place; you cannot avoid him. We collide with him every moment.

It is just because we have some idea of God we go on missing him. We have some idea that he is somewhere far away in heaven; hence we go on missing him. Drop that stupid idea and you will find him everywhere. He is very close by.

Once, Ramakrishna was asked, "Where is God?" And he said, "You tell me where he is not. I have been searching for the place where he is not and I have failed. I have not yet found a place where he is not."

MONTH 2

Say 'yes'

Peolple are miserable because they have decided to resist existence.

From this moment on don't resist. Relax, let go. Let existence take charge of the whole of your life, and then life has a totally different flavour. Then bliss is as natural as breathing.

day **2**

Everything is a gift from existence. We don't deserve anything, we are not worthy of anything. Existence gives us life, the capacity to love, the capacity to feel beauty, the capacity to find truth – not because we are worthy, not because we deserve them, but because it has too much.

It is like a cloud full of rain: it has to shower. It is out of its abundance that we receive. It is like a flower that has inexhaustible perfume – it is bound to be released to the winds. It is like a light – beginningless, endless. It has to be shared; otherwise it becomes a burden.

CONTEMPLATION BEFORE SLEEP

B liss is not something that has to happen some-where in the future; it is already the case. We have simply become disconnected with it. It is still there as an undercurrent but you have forgotten how to connect yourself with it. You have become unplugged – and my whole work is to plug you in again to an undercurrent of joy, bliss, peace, love, harmony.

Meditation is only a method to reconnect you, to give you some idea where to reach your own nature.

d
a
y
4

Life is a gift, birth is a gift, love is a gift, death is a gift. If we know how to appreciate, all is a gift; if we don't know how to appreciate then there is nothing but complaints and complaints in life.

There are only two types of people. Those who know how to appreciate the beauty of that which is, of that which has been given to them: And those who have no sense of appreciation; they are always condemning, complaining, asking for more and more.

Only the first kind of people can become religious, the second kind cannot become religious. The second kind is bound to deny God sooner or later, because God becomes an enemy who is not fulfilling your desires. It is these people who have made the proverb "Man proposes and God disposes."

The proverb is made by non-religious people. They are always feeling frustrated, whatsoever happens is wrong. It is never up to the mark, it is never fulfilling, never to their heart's content; it is always falling short. They live in misery because there is always a grudge, as if they are deprived of something. How can they feel grateful? And without gratefulness there is no prayer, without prayer there is no religion.

CONTEMPLATION BEFORE SLEEP

Prayer is praising the Lord for all that is. It is an approach of a yes-saying heart which knows no doubt, no scepticism, no negativity, which can dance and sing because the world is so beautiful. It is a gift of which we are not worthy. We cannot repay the lord; all that we can do is praise. We can sing hallelujah! And if one becomes a full 'hallelujah' nothing else is needed. Then everything is possible, then even the impossible is possible.

So let prayer be your path. Praise in as many ways as possible, and never complain. Drop the complaining mind. And it is only a question of decision. Once it is decided, one starts dropping the old habit of complaining and the whole energy starts moving in praise. Praise brings blessings, benediction. Praise in all possible ways: praise the sunset, and the clouds, and the trees, and the birds and the people. Don't be a miser in praising. Praise wholeheartedly, as totally as possible, and it will bring you closer and closer to existence. It will become the bridge. It is the shortest route to existence. Meditation is a long route, prayer is a short-cut.

*d
a
y*

6

Prayer is the foundation of religion, and it is prayer realized that becomes the experience of existence. The seed of prayer is gratitude. Feel grateful, because great is the gift of existence and it is constantly showering on you, but we start taking it for granted. That is one of the most stupid things that a human being can do, but the mind is always doing it; it starts taking things for granted.

The sun rises, the dawn has tremendous beauty, but your mind says, "So what? It happens every day. It is just another morning, just like others." The whole of the east is red with the rising sun and the clouds are full of colour, but the mind says, "So what? It is nothing new. Millions of times it has happened and millions of times it is going to happen again."

If this is the way of looking at things, and this is how mind looks at things, it becomes insensitive – insensitive to beauty, insensitive to music, insensitive to poetry, insensitive to love, insensitive to everything that is valuable. Then naturally you live in darkness, you live in ugliness. It is your own creation.

Start feeling grateful. Grow the sense of appreciation. Praise existence for what has already been done and then much more will go on happening to you. The more you praise, the more you become capable of seeing, the more perceptive you become. A prayerful person becomes so perceptive that he sees existence everywhere, he finds its signature everywhere – scriptures in silence, sermons in stones.

CONTEMPLATION BEFORE SLEEP

Just dissolve yourself into a loving energy, just become a loving energy – not in love with something in particular, but just having love for each and everything, even for nothing! It is not a question of an object for love, but just of an overflowing, loving energy.

If you are sitting silently in your room, let the room be full of loving energy, create an aura of love around yourself. If you are looking at the trees, you are in love with the trees. If you are looking at the stars, you are in love with the stars. You are love, that's all. So wherever you are, go on pouring your love onto...rocks. And when you pour love onto rocks even rocks are no longer rocks.

Love is such a miracle, such magic, that it transforms everything into the beloved. You become love and existence becomes your beloved, existence becomes God.

People seek and search for God without becoming love. How can they find him? They don't have the necessary equipment, the necessary context and space.

Create love and forget all about God. Suddenly one day you will encounter him everywhere.

d a y

8

Be as silent as possible. Sit more and more in stillness – not only in bodily stillness. That too is helpful and creates a situation, but it is not the end, it is just the beginning. It is more important that the mind should be still, that the mind should stop its constant chattering. And it does stop – we have just never tried.

All that is needed is a very simple process: you sit inside yourself and watch. Let the mind do all kinds of old tricks and you simply watch non-judgementally, neither saying good nor bad, neither choosing nor rejecting – utterly indifferent, cool. Slowly slowly, the knack is learned by remaining cool and indifferent.

First the mind tries all its old tricks, and then by and by it starts feeling embarrassed because you are not getting affected in any way, this way or that. Even if you become affected by it, then too the mind is perfectly at ease; it has disturbed you. So don't be against it, don't fight with it, and don't fall a victim to its tricks. Just remain aloof.

Many times you will get involved. The moment you remember, pull yourself out. Again compose yourself, again start watching. A thought arises – see it. It comes in front of you – see it. Then it passes by. Take note of it, with no idea of whether it is good or bad, whether it should be or should not be, with no moral attitude, just a scientific, cool observation.

One day, suddenly, it is not there, and that day such a silence descends as you have never known before. Then it never leaves you; it remains with you, becomes your very soul. It is very liberating.

CONTEMPLATION BEFORE SLEEP

Be more and more silent. Whenever you have the opportunity, just sit silently doing nothing, not even meditation. Just sit silently for no reason, for no purpose. Slowly slowly, silence grows, it becomes an overwhelming experience. And when silence has permeated you through and through, you will know who you are and you will know what this life is all about. In knowing it one knows God.

d
a
y
10

Before death takes over, the real home has to be found. And it can be found because it is not far away. It can be found because it is exactly within your being. You have not even to travel a little bit; on the contrary, you have to sit silently and drop all kinds of mental travels.

When the mind is not moving in the past or in the future, travelling stops. And in that very moment, the seed starts growing into a plant. Then there are infinite possibilities – the fruits, the flowers, the sun and the winds and the rain, and then you can feel enjoyment.

You can dance with the wind, you can share joy with the clouds, you can whisper with the stars.

CONTEMPLATION BEFORE SLEEP

The door to the divine is spontaneity. To be spontaneous is to be in godliness. Mind is never spontaneous. It is either in the past or in the future, either in that which is no more or in that which is not yet. Between these two it goes on missing that which is, and that is the door.

The present moment is not part of time; hence the present moment is not available to mind either. Mind and time are synonymous. You can say that mind is time inside your being, and time is mind outside you, but they are one phenomenon.

The present moment is neither part of time nor part of mind. When you are in the present moment, you are in godliness. That is the true meaning of meditation, the true meaning of prayer, the true meaning of love. And when one acts out of the present moment, that action is never binding because it is not your action, it is godliness acting through you. It is godliness flowing through you.

d
a
y

12

Drop all boundaries, become infinite. Think only in terms of infinity, eternity. Less than that has never satisfied anybody and is not going to satisfy anybody – ever.

The boundary of the body has to be dropped. We are too identified with our bodies. We think that we are the body, and we are not. This is the first falsehood that has to be dropped. Out of this falsehood many other falsehoods arise. If one is identified with the body then one will be afraid of old age, disease, death. They grow out of this identification with the body.

Think of yourself as pure consciousness. You are not the body, you are the one who is aware of the body. And you are not the mind either.

First start working with the body because it is easier to start with the gross. Then move to the subtle: look at the mind as separate from yourself. As you become aware that you are neither the body nor the mind, you will feel great freedom arising in you, unhindered. There will be no obstruction, no walls, but in all directions open space. Then the most subtle barrier has to be dropped – that of feeling. That is the subtlest. First body, then mind, then heart; and to be free from the heart is to be enlightened.

When you know you are neither the body nor the mind nor the heart you immediately know who you are, and what existence is and what this life is all about. All the secrets are immediately revealed.

CONTEMPLATION BEFORE SLEEP

We are all strangers here. This is not our home, our home is somewhere else. We are in a foreign land. To remain outside oneself is to remain homeless; to come in is to be back home. Now every effort has to be made to come in. No stone is to be left unturned. Everything has to be risked, because nothing is more precious than this turning in. Everything can be lost for it, sacrificed for it, because all else is trivia.

day
13

The religious person lives egolessly. He knows, "I am part of the whole, an intrinsic part of the whole, not at all separate." To know it, that "I am not separate from the whole," brings tremendous freedom. It brings vastness, the whole sky is yours. You are no longer identified with a small, very small ego.

We are vast but we have become confined in small spaces; that's why there is so much misery. It is like forcing an ocean into a dewdrop. We are birds with wings who need to have the whole sky, but are encaged. Nobody is encaging us, but the irony is we go on encaging ourselves. We are the prison, and we are the prisoner and we are the jailer – there is nobody else. That's why the mystics call it a dream – it is a dream. The moment you wake up you find that: "This is strange. I was chased by a lion, but I was the lion and I was chased. And I was the spectator too, the witness to the whole thing!" This is how life is, like a dream.

Now it is time.... If children play with stupid games they can be forgiven. They need to go astray, they need to commit many mistakes. But as you grow older you cannot be forgiven. And the ego is the most stupid game because it is against reality, it is against existence. We go on creating our own prisons out of our imagination, our desire, our memory, our ambition, our jealousy. And they all go on spinning subtle structures around us. The whole structure is called the ego. The whole work of the mind is called the ego. From this very moment become aware of it, and slowly slowly get out of it.

CONTEMPLATION BEFORE SLEEP

Ego is our hell, and the irony is that we are the creators of it. We create it and we suffer. But it is within our capacity not to create it and to move away from suffering. The moment the ego is not there and the suffering is not there, you are in bliss. Bliss is our nature; suffering is a created phenomenon, arbitrary. Bliss is uncreated: it is there right now, underneath suffering, like an undercurrent. You need not create it, it is already the case – just don't create suffering. And the secret of creating suffering is in the formula of the ego.

Being a sannyasin means dropping the ego. From this first moment don't think of yourself as superior, or as inferior; both are ego attitudes. Don't think of yourself as somebody or as nobody; both are ego attitudes. Try to understand the cunningness of the ego; it can even become humble, it can say, "I am humble, there is nobody more humble than me."

It has come in from the back door.

d a y

16

Ego consists of feeling, of thinking that we are separate from existence, that we are like islands. It is absolutely false. We don't exist in separation, we can't exist even for a single moment in separation. The breath that comes in keeps us joined with the outside. And we are not only breathing with the nose, we are breathing from every pore of the body.

We are thirsty – we drink water and the water quenches the thirst. It is continuously moving from the outer towards the inner and from the inner towards the outer. Food is continuously in circulation, breathing is in circulation. We are in constant exchange with reality. We are not separate, we are bridged in a thousand and one ways.

CONTEMPLATION BEFORE SLEEP

The ego can exist only if you fight. Surrender is poison to the ego; hence the emphasis on surrender. Fight is food; surrender is poison. And the ego has to die, only then can you be born.

In one sheath there can't be two swords. Either you can live inside yourself and the ego goes, or the ego lives and you have to go underground. That's how millions of people are – living underground lives, and the egos are sitting on the throne. In surrender the ego disappears and your underground self starts surfacing back to its natural status, its natural state.

Your life can be an instrument of existence, a bamboo flute on its lips. You just have to be hollow and let it sing the song if it wants. Or if it does not want, then silence is as beautiful as the song.

d a y
18

The man who has never known anything of meditation lives a barren life, just like a desert.

I have heard about an American tourist dressed in his swimsuit running towards the ocean, perspiring. He met a man and he asked, "How far is the ocean?" The man looked at the American, felt very sorry for him and said, "It will be difficult to reach it – this is the Sahara and the ocean is at least eight hundred miles away from here." The American said, "Then I will have to rest here on the beach!"

You can believe your desert to be a beach. That's how people are living, believing their desert is a beach. It is simply desert. At least in the Sahara, after eight hundred miles, you will find the ocean, but in a life without meditation the Sahara is unending. Not even after eight hundred miles....

CONTEMPLATION BEFORE SLEEP

Bliss is never our achievement. It cannot be because it happens only when we have disappeared. If we are still there to claim that we have achieved it, it is a pseudo bliss, it is not true, it is just a dream; soon it will be gone and you will fall back into misery.

Mind has played a trick on you, and mind is very cunning, very political, very diplomatic. It goes on finding ways and means to keep you hanging around it. And the ultimate trick, the last trick that it can play is to create a false sense of bliss.

The real bliss is always a gift from existence, and it can happen only when the ego dies. The ego is the barrier. The moment you are not, existence is, and the experience of existence happening in your total silence and nothingness is bliss. That dance of existence in your absolutely silent space, with nothing to interfere – no mind, no ego to distort it, to hamper it, to hinder it – that is bliss.

The work of meditation is negative. It is to destroy the ego. Then bliss comes on its own.

d
a
y

20

Meditation means becoming nobody. It means dissolving yourself into the whole – not keeping your separation, not resisting, but dissolving...a love affair with the whole, an orgasmic unity with the whole. And of course, before the whole we are nothing – small, like dewdrops before the ocean. And the moment you know that you are nothing compared to the whole, you accept it joyfully – not in resignation but rejoicing, rejoicing because with the ego disappear all anxieties, all fears.

Even the fear of death disappears the moment you drop the ego, because only the ego dies. Your reality is eternal.

When all anxieties, worries have gone, you are left in total rest.

Egolessness is the beginning of meditation, and rest is the fulfilment. When you are so deeply restful that nothing stirs in you, you have come home...what in the East has been known as *satchitanand*: truth, consciousness, bliss – the three faces of God, the real Trinity.

The moment you are totally peaceful, still, all those three faces are yours – you become divine. In fact you have always been divine, but now you discover it.

CONTEMPLATION BEFORE SLEEP

Meditate so that prayer can happen. And the only proof that the prayer has happened is that you will experience the fragrance, and others will experience the fragrance of your experience. You will radiate it. You will be it, and whatsoever you touch will start dancing with joy. Even dust is transformed into gold by the touch of a man who knows what prayer is.

Prayer is sheer magic – but it comes out of meditation, never otherwise. Hence, here my insistence is on meditation, not on prayer, because I know prayer is inevitable. If meditation happens, prayer is inevitable. If prayer is there, fragrance is a natural consequence.

So I don't teach prayer, I don't teach service to humanity, because I know that meditation is all that is needed. Once meditation is there, everything follows in its own time, in the right time. Prayer comes, and out of prayer, service to humanity – that's its fragrance.

d
a
y

22

A prayer without meditation is false because it depends on beliefs; you have to believe in a God you know not. And how can you really pray to a God you know not? You can deceive others and yourself, but prayer cannot arise out of belief; that would be basically dishonest. And if even prayer is dishonest, what can be honest in life?

But there are millions of people in the world who know nothing of meditation and still go on praying. They are carrying plastic flowers believing that they are real roses. Hence they go on praying but their whole life has no fragrance of prayer. On the contrary, their life stinks of all kinds of jealousies, hatreds, violence, greediness. There seems to be no fragrance at all.

My own observation is that a real religion begins in meditation.

Meditation means a state of thoughtless silence. And when you are absolutely silent with no thought disturbing your silence, stirring it, the joy of such a silence is so tremendous that you are bound to thank the universe. It is impossible not to, it is impossible not to feel grateful. It is not a question of belief anymore; you know the bliss, you have experienced the silence, the music of it, and out of the music your heart is full of prayerfulness. You bow to existence.

CONTEMPLATION BEFORE SLEEP

Prayer is nothing but silence, pure silence. You are not saying anything to anybody; the other is absolutely absent. There is no content in your consciousness, not even a small ripple in the lake of consciousness; all is still and silent.

Nothing is said, but the heart, the beat of the heart, the flow of the blood, the very grace that surrounds that silence and a tremendous wish to bow down to the whole existence for all that it has done for us, is prayer. Hence I don't teach prayer here, I only teach silence; because prayer is a necessary outcome of silence, is a flowering of silence. You work to create silence, and when your work is complete prayer arrives.

It is just like spring coming, and the trees are full of flowers. Create silence and you have created the spring. Now the flowers are not far away, they are bound to come. Create silence and you will be blessed by prayer.

d
a
y
24

Bliss is beloved of all. Whatsoever we are doing, we are searching for bliss. In every act – right or wrong, moral or immoral, material or spiritual – the search is the same, the search for the ultimate beloved – and that is bliss.

And the moment that you are totally still and silent it wells up within your being. That moment is the moment when one is really born. Before that, one is only physiologically born, not spiritually. We do not have a soul before that. Only after that does one become a soul, does one become immortal, does one become a God.

CONTEMPLATION BEFORE SLEEP

A man of awareness, a meditative person, is never distracted because he watches everything. He will watch the phone ringing, he will watch the child crying, he will watch the neighbours and their radio getting louder and louder – he has nothing to do with it. He is cool and calm and open from all sides. So whatsoever happens – if the train whistles, the aeroplane passes over, or there is a distant call of the cuckoo – everything is included.

It is a knack. If you go on doing it, slowly slowly the knack is learned. And the moment you have learned the knack of meditation you are a new being. It is a new birth, the real birth, because in that very moment you know you are neither the body nor the mind, you are pure consciousness. In that very moment you know that this pure consciousness was before birth, and is going to remain after death. It is immortal.

This is the discovery of immortality. And to discover immortality is to discover eternity.

Learn how to disappear, how to evaporate. Learn how not to be. That is the greatest art in life because the ego is so cunning.

It always finds some way to come in from the back door. It can become humble, it can become pious, it can become saintly, it can become holy. It can play all kinds of games.

Be watchful. And the more you know the ways of the ego, the more you are free of it, because it can no longer play upon you whatsoever strategy you have come to know. Slowly slowly all doors are closed. One day, when the last strategy has collapsed, you are freed from yourself.

That is liberation. And that is the ultimate goal of all religious effort. Only in that liberated state can one know what truth is. They are not really two separate things, but two aspects of the same coin. Liberation is truth.

CONTEMPLATION BEFORE SLEEP

Make it a point now to give more and more emphasis to the inner, more and more time and space to the inner. And it is only a question of remembering.

Slowly slowly your consciousness takes a turn. And when you start facing yourself, you are facing the greatest phenomenon, the most exquisite, the most beautiful experience of life, because you are seeing life in its intrinsic grace and splendour.

day
28

Man is born with a very small flame of godliness within him, but it is hidden behind layers and layers of darkness.

So whenever one enters oneself, first one has to pass through a jungle of darkness – and that's what scares many people. Many people try to go in but then they escape again, because that darkness makes them really afraid. It looks like death.

The Christian mystics have given it the right name: the dark night of the soul. But one has to pass through the dark night; otherwise there is no dawn. The dark night is the womb for the dawn. The master is really needed to help you while you are passing through the darkness. Once you have seen your own light there is no need for any help. You are grateful to the master, but you have come home, the journey is over.

CONTEMPLATION BEFORE SLEEP

Whenever you have time, forget the outer; it is superficial.

Dive deep into the inner, and you will find the light, the light that is our very life, the light that is the stuff we are made of and of which the whole universe is also made.

In the old days that stuff was called God. Now that word has become a little dangerous. People don't like that word; it looks a little old-fashioned. It smells of priesthood, churches, and the smell is not good.

So I don't say you will encounter God within. But I can't help it, you will! That light is what God is. And unless one knows that one is something eternal which cannot be destroyed by anything, one remains on the circumference, accidental.

*d
a
y*

30

Religion is nothing but the simple art of dissolving yourself into the whole. The whole is called God.

That's why the man who has attained to God is called holy. He has become whole, he is no longer separate, he has dropped that stupid idea of being separate. He is no longer like an ice cube, he has melted and merged into the ocean.

That moment is the moment of great bliss. And after that one can never fall from bliss – there is no way to fall. Even if one wants to be miserable, one cannot be.

The ordinary person who lives like an ego tries hard to be blissful but he cannot be; he remains miserable. And the surrendered person, even if he tries to be miserable, cannot be. Bliss is the consequence of surrender; and misery the consequence of resistance.

CONTEMPLATION BEFORE SLEEP

Once your inner light is found your life is nothing but pure bliss. It is not only bliss for yourself, it becomes contagious, it starts affecting other people. Those who are receptive will start feeling something when they are close to you. Their hearts will respond, some bells will start ringing in their beings...a kind of synchronicity.

One man becoming blissful can trigger a process in thousands of people. Hence my interest is not in the society, but in individuals. If I can transform a few thousand people, that will do – they will ignite thousands more. And it is an unending process, it goes on and on.

MONTH 3

Jump from darkness to light

Man is not as small as he appears from the outside. He contains the whole sky within, he contains all the oceans. Yes, he looks like a dewdrop, but his appearance is very deceptive. And science is still working on his appearance, the dewdrop.

Those who have penetrated deeper into human consciousness were surprised to find that as you go deeper, man becomes vast. When you reach his very core, he is the whole universe. And that is the experience of godliness.

Meditate and go deeper inwards. It is already there – we just have to uncover it.

CONTEMPLATION BEFORE SLEEP

Anything that brings bliss to you is a nourishment to the soul. And it is not only that people's bodies are starving, their souls are starving far more.

Be alert: choose bliss as much as possible. Avoid misery; never cooperate with any misery that surrounds you sometimes. It's bound to surround you, just like clouds come one day and another day it is sunny.

Watch the clouds, watch the sun, and remember that you are separate from both. Dark moments come, light moments come – we are moving on a wheel of day and night, birth and death, summer and winter. But if we can remember that we are not any of these, then bliss arises. Then one is suddenly at peace with oneself and at peace with existence. That is bliss – that harmony, that accord, that attunement.

And once you have learned to be blissful, your soul starts growing. Otherwise it remains a seed, it never becomes a tree. And unless the seed becomes a tree and the tree blooms and brings much fruit, life is a wastage.

d
a
y
3

A blissful person is incapable of doing wrong to anybody – to himself or to others. He simply becomes incapable of doing wrong. But the miserable person is bound to do wrong. He may think that he is trying to do something good, but he can't do good. Even though he has the intention of doing good, the outcome is not going to be good.

He may think that he loves people but he will simply dominate in the name of love. He may think that he is a great servant of the people but he will simply be a politician; through service he will try to dominate. The miserable person is basically impotent at doing good.

Hence, to me, virtue can be reduced to one thing, that is blissfulness. And sin can be reduced to one thing, that is misery. Misery is sin, and bliss is virtue.

My only message to sannyasins is: be cheerful, be blissful, be dancing, be singing, and then whatsoever you do is going to be right.

CONTEMPLATION BEFORE SLEEP

Bliss is only for those who are courageous, daring, brave, because bliss happens only when you have moved beyond the known into the unknown. Whenever you become confined to the known, your life becomes routine, repetitive. It goes on moving in the same rut, it goes around in circles, and slowly slowly it dulls all your sensitivities, all your receptivities.

It hardens people. It makes them blind, it makes them deaf, it makes them dumb, because there is nothing to see and nothing to hear and nothing to taste and nothing to feel. They have known it all; it is the same repetition. How can there be bliss in such a life? Such a life has only one taste – that of misery, depression, a sadness, a settled sadness.

But if one is courageous enough to move continuously from the known into the unknown, from the familiar into the unfamiliar....

It is risky, because the familiar is secure, safe. And who knows what is going to happen if you go into the unknown, into the uncharted? You take your small boat and you go into the uncharted sea. Who knows if you will ever come back to the old shore again? Who can give you a guarantee? There is no guarantee. But unless one is ready to live in such a dangerous state one cannot remain blissful. Live dangerously – because life knows no other way: it has to be lived dangerously.

For the sannyasin, courage is the greatest virtue, and then bliss goes on happening. If one is ready to live dangerously, many flowers of bliss are going to bloom.

d
a
y
5

The greatest courage in the world is to not imitate others, to live one's own life as authentically as possible, whatsoever the cost. Even if life is lost in living your own life it is worth it, because that is how the soul is born. When one is ready to die for something, in that very agony – the word 'agony' means struggle – in that very struggle one is born. It is a birth pain. It takes courage, it takes guts.

Live your life without being bothered by the moralists, puritans, priests, stupid people who go on advising. Live *your* life. Even if you live in error, then too it is better to live your own life than to be right according to somebody else, because the man who is right according to somebody else is false, and the man who is wrong according to his own decision is going to learn from his error sooner or later. He will grow out of it, he will be benefited by it.

The only person who learns is the person who is ready to commit errors, and the best way to commit errors is not to listen to others – just go on doing your thing!

CONTEMPLATION BEFORE SLEEP

day **6**

Life is for the courageous. The coward only vegetates. The coward goes on hesitating, and by the time he decides, the moment is lost. The coward only thinks to live but never lives, thinks to love but never loves. And the world is full of cowards. The coward has a basic fear, the fear of the unknown. He keeps himself within the boundaries of the known, of the familiar. Courage begins when you step beyond the boundaries of the known. It is risking – it is dangerous. But the more you risk, the more you are. The more you accept the challenge of the unknown, the more integrated you become. It is only in tremendous danger that the soul is born; otherwise the person remains just the body.

For millions of people the soul is only a possibility, not a reality. Only a very few, courageous ones have been soul-full.

day 7

The two qualities of being courageous and being blissful prepare the ground for God to descend in you. You have to be courageous because God is unknown. And whatsoever you have heard about God, when you really come to know God you will be surprised. All that you heard about him was sheer nonsense, bullshit!

There is no way to describe the experience. God remains indefinable, inexpressible. It is so unknown that even those who have experienced him cannot relate their experience to anybody else; one simply remains dumb.

The English word 'mystic' is very beautiful. Its original meaning is: one who has become dumb through experiencing, one who has come across such a truth that he can only say it is mysterious, that it is a mystery – which is saying nothing.

CONTEMPLATION BEFORE SLEEP

When you are climbing towards the heights, reaching towards God – because that is the only true height, everything else is far below – when you are trying to reach towards God, you become the ascending one. And the miracle is that when you start ascending towards God, God starts descending towards you.

The meeting always happens somewhere in between, it is not one way. It is not only that the seeker moves towards God, the moment the seeker starts moving, God starts moving; it is simultaneous. It is in fact one process and there are two polarities of the one process – the seeker and the sought; it is one phenomenon. But God cannot descend in you unless you start ascending.

People go on living as if this mundane life is all there is. People go on living as if there is nothing higher possible. There is immense possibility. Man comes with a great potential. The ultimate height of every man's being is God.

It is not only that man is seeking God, God is also seeking man. If it were only a one-way affair it would not be so beautiful, it would be cold from the other side. It is not so. It is a hot love affair.

day **9**

Life is a divine story. It is not your biography, it is God's biography.

We are simply pages in it, paragraphs in it, footnotes in it.

Existence is a great orchestra; we are small notes, small instruments. We can play in tune with the whole – that brings bliss. We can play against the whole – that brings misery. It is as simple as that.

So whenever you feel miserable remember that knowingly or unknowingly you are doing something against the whole. Put it right.

Nobody is responsible except you, take the whole responsibility on yourself. And whenever you feel blissful, learn from that moment. You must have fallen in tune with the whole. So remember how it happened, and create the same contact again and again so that it can happen more and it can happen more deeply.

Misery and bliss are great teachers. If we can simply watch and learn from these two teachers no other scripture is needed.

CONTEMPLATION BEFORE SLEEP

Before bliss can happen, you have to become integrated like a rock. People are like sand, just thousands of fragments, a crowd, a multitude; they are not one. And bliss can happen only when you are one, otherwise your inner crowd will go on creating noise, conflict, struggle, tension, anguish.

The whole crowd has to be melted into one unity. When that integration happens, bliss naturally comes as a by-product. Bliss is a by-product of inner integrity, and the rock represents integration.

day

11

The whole existence is surrounded by a divine energy that protects you, cares for you, is always available. If you go on missing it, it is only because of you.

If you keep your doors closed, the sun may be outside but you will live in darkness. Even if the doors are open and the sun is there, you can keep your eyes closed and you will still live in darkness.

So is the case with God: his love is always there, but our hearts are not open, our hearts are closed.

Make your heart available to God so that you can receive, so that you can pulsate with the whole, in accord with the whole. And then great benediction is yours.

CONTEMPLATION BEFORE SLEEP

Meditators are bound to be more intelligent than other people. If they are not then their meditation is false, then they don't know what meditation is; they are doing something else in the name of meditation.

A meditative person is bound to be more sensitive, more intelligent, more creative, more loving, more compassionate. These qualities grow of their own accord. And the whole secret is in one thing: learn to stop the mind.

The moment you know how to stop the mind, you become the master, and then the mind is a beautiful mechanism. You use it when you want to use it, when it is needed, and you put it off when it is not needed.

Become more and more aware of all that you think, of all that you desire, imagine, dream. Just remember that you have to be conscious of everything. Walking, be conscious of it; eating, be conscious of it; thinking, go on watching what thoughts are passing in the mind. One day you will be surprised, when you have learned the knack of it, it continues even in sleep. You go on watching the dreams. You know what kind of dreams are passing by, and you know that they are dreams.

That day, when one can watch one's own dreams, is a great transformation. From that moment onwards you are a new being. Then you enter into the world of reality.

By watching dreams, thoughts, desires, slowly slowly we become the watcher, we become disidentified with all that we are watching, we become the witness. And that witness is the ultimate reality.

CONTEMPLATION BEFORE SLEEP

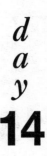

My essential message is: don't live out of fear, because there is no question of being punished. Live fearlessly because only then do you live totally.

Fear naturally closes you, it does not allow you to open up. You have to consider a thousand and one things before you can do a single thing – whether it is right or wrong, moral or immoral, according to the church or not, whether the scriptures favour it or are against it. And you will get more and more confused the more you think about it. Once you start moving in that direction of making things into sins, you cannot live, you only drag yourself along.

My approach is totally different. There are mistakes, but there is no sin at all. Only one thing has to be remembered: don't commit the same error again and again because that is stupid. One should explore life, and in exploring, sometimes you go astray. If you are too afraid of going astray, you cannot explore. Then the whole adventure of life is crushed, killed, destroyed. And that's what so-called religious people have done: they have made religion so serious, so sombre, they have given religion such a long face.

My effort is to give you joy, gusto for life, courage to adventure, to move fearlessly, exploring all possibilities that life makes available, fearless in expanding and being open and vulnerable. Because God is our judge we need not be afraid. Finally at the judgement day when you see God, you can tell him, "Yes, I have been drinking...please forgive me. I have tried a few other things also." And I think he will understand. Don't be worried!

day 15

It is hard to drop the old, but it has to be dropped because only then is the new possible. It is hard to accept the new because it is new and we are unfamiliar with it. It is a stranger, and deep down we are apprehensive and afraid. But one has to learn to love the new; otherwise there is no growth possible.

Growth simply means the courage to drop the old, and the courage to love the new. And this is not to be done only once, it has to be done every moment, because every moment something is becoming old and something new is knocking at the door. Whenever that is happening, listen to the new and become utterly deaf to the old.

The old functions as a bondage, the new brings freedom. Truth is always new. God is always fresh, as fresh as the dewdrops in the early morning sun.

CONTEMPLATION BEFORE SLEEP

Truth is not available ready-made. It is neither in the traditions nor in the scriptures. It has to be inquired into, explored, and everyone has to inquire into it. I may have found it but I cannot give it to you. It is not that I don't want to give it to you, but it is untransferable. It simply can't be given; there is no way to give it. The moment you give it, it becomes a lie. You have to discover it on your own.

Buddhas can show the way, but you will have to travel the whole journey. It is a long, arduous journey but tremendously beautiful. Each moment is full of surprise, each moment is so full of wonder.

d
a
y

17

Truth is available only to the innocent conscious-ness – a consciousness which is as innocent as a child, a consciousness which knows nothing. When you know, your mirror is full of dust – knowledge gathers dust like a mirror. When you don't know anything, you are full of wonder and awe, your mirror is clean. And that clean mirror reflects the truth.

CONTEMPLATION BEFORE SLEEP

Truth is not something which has to be achieved, it is already inside us. We are it – the seeker is the sought. But we go on rushing hither and thither searching for the truth. We will never find it anywhere else; hence the only way to find it is to stop seeking it outside.

The only way to find it is to sit silently and look within. It is not a question of doing something, it is more a question of not doing anything.

When you are in a state of non-doing, utterly relaxed, it happens, it wells up. It has always been there but you have never been there. The meeting happens when you are also inside yourself.

A lamp is burning there within you. It has always been there; we just never look at it. We are keeping our back towards it; hence we live in darkness.

Darkness is our own creation. If we turn inwards, all is light; if we look out, all is dark. Darkness simply means that we have become focused on the outside and forgotten the inner world.

Light is our very nature, and light is the nature of the whole existence. Existence consists of light, it is made of light. That's why all the scriptures of the world say God is light. And now, modern science also agrees that the universe is made of electricity, electrons. Those are scientific terms; light is a more poetic term.

So make a decision that from now onwards you have to make all effort to turn inwards.

CONTEMPLATION BEFORE SLEEP

We are born of light, we live in light, we die in light – we are made out of light. This has been one of the greatest insights of the mystics of all the ages. The scientists have also agreed to it just now, within these twenty years; they had to agree. Just twenty years ago they were laughing at the mystics, thinking that they were talking nonsense – "Man made of light? They must be talking metaphorically, not literally." But mystics were really talking literally.

Now, science not only says that man is made of light but that everything is made of light, all is made of electrons, electricity. Science has come to this understanding from a very very long route. The objective route is a very long route; the subjective route is very easy, the shortest possible, because you have only to look within. Nothing else is required: no lab, no instruments, no sophisticated devices, nothing else is required – just the art of closing your eyes and looking inwards.

That's what meditation is: the art of looking inwards. And the moment thoughts disappear and the mind is utterly quiet and silent, the inner light is seen. That is a revelation.

And once you have seen your light, you will be surprised: you can then see it in everybody else. Then the whole existence is nothing but an ocean of light. It is not matter, it is pure energy.

day **21**

For centuries, God has been thought of as light. That is because of our fear of darkness. Not that God is only light, God is as much light as he is darkness.

God has to be both; otherwise darkness would not exist at all. God has to be the lowest and the highest, matter and mind. God has to be the whole, and the whole contains the polar opposite. God cannot be only light.

It is because of our fear of darkness that we have never thought of God as dark. And to approach God through fear is not right. God should be approached fearlessly, in deep love.

If you look with fear you will project your fear. You will see things which are not there and you will not see things which are there. When you are not afraid you look with absolute clarity. Fear is like smoke surrounding you, like clouds. And God can be seen only with clarity, absolute clarity, unconditional clarity, clarity and nothing else.

Then God is both – he is as much light as dark. Then he is both summer and winter, life and death. Then the duality disappears and a tremendous oneness arises in your vision.

We are bound by the dual and we can be freed only by the one. As Plotinus says: "The search for God is a flight of the alone to the alone."

Start looking at darkness as divine. Start looking at everything as divine, because all is divine whether we know it or not, whether we recognize it or not. Our recognition is irrelevant – existence is divine. If we recognize it, we rejoice; if we don't recognize it, we suffer unnecessarily.

CONTEMPLATION BEFORE SLEEP

Man appears very finite, very small, just like a dewdrop. But he contains all the oceans in him, he contains all the skies in him. If you look from the outside he is very small, tiny; just dust, nothing much – dust unto dust. But if you look from the inside, from his centre, he is the whole universe.

That's the difference between science and religion: science looks at man from the outside and finds nothing spiritual, nothing divine, just physiology, chemistry, biology – another kind of animal.

Hence scientists go on studying animals to understand man. Animals are more simple, easily manipulatable, so scientists go on researching on rats. And whatsoever they conclude, they go on insisting that this is the case with humanity. It is a little more complex of course, but basically it is the same. Science has reduced man to rats. And man can only be understood now by studying rats or dogs.

Man has to be understood only by understanding Buddhas, Christs, Krishnas. Always remember that this is one of the fundamentals, you cannot understand the higher by understanding the lower, but you can understand the lower by understanding the higher. The higher contains the lower but the lower does not contain the higher.

The only way to understand man is not from the outside, not through observation, but through meditation. One has to enter into one's interiority, into one's own subjectivity. Standing there one comes to know the greatest wonder and the utmost awe – that man is nothing but God.

Science goes on telling people: "You are nothing but animals. Human beings are only a species of animal." And for three hundred years they have been propagating the idea. It has penetrated very deeply into our blood and bones and marrow.

We are not animals. In fact, animals themselves are not animals. We are divine, so are the animals. Religion is rooted in this vision of man being divine, of the universe being divine. Science reduces everything to the lowest common denominator. If you bring a lotus flower to the scientist he will say that it is nothing but mud because it grows in mud, it comes out of mud. If you bring mud to a mystic he will say, "Don't be worried – there are thousands of lotuses hidden in it, because lotuses grow out of mud."

Religion looks from the highest point and makes the highest point the decisive factor. Science looks at the lowest and makes that the decisive factor.

From this moment this has to be your vision: you are divine, so is the whole universe. With that vision it is easy to move upwards, because if there is no upwards, no possibility of anything higher, then one forgets all about transforming oneself. If there is a possibility one starts groping for it. The possibility is there. The buddhas are enough proof of it, enough evidence for it.

CONTEMPLATION BEFORE SLEEP

Everyone is God. Nobody can be anything else because only God exists. God is synonymous with existence. To be means to be a God. But we don't remember it, we are absolutely oblivious to it. So the question is not how to achieve godhood, the question is how to remember it. It is a forgotten language.

My effort here is to help you to remember something that is already there. Nothing has to be achieved. You have only to discover yourself, to discover who you are, and you will know that you are God.

And the moment you know you are God, the whole existence becomes divine, then everybody is a God. And that is a tremendous joy, when the whole existence looks divine to you. You are surrounded by gods. Naturally, great rejoicing arises in your heart.

day **25**

Man is a bridge between the animal world and the world of the gods. Man is just in between, he is a passage; hence man is not really a being. A lion has a certain being, a rosebush has a certain being, a rock has a certain being. Man has none.

Man is a becoming, not a being. Man becomes a being only when he has transcended humanity, when he has become a Buddha, a Christ. Then he attains to being, but then he is no more man. He has passed over the bridge.

Pass over the bridge. Remember, don't make your house on the bridge. It is something to be passed over, something to be transcended. And that is the beauty of man. No dog can be anything other than a dog; no rock can be anything other than a rock. They have a fixed being; there is no possibility of growth.

Only man grows. Only man has the possibility of adventure, of journeying into the unknown. The greatest beauty of man, the greatest grandeur, is that he can surpass himself. It looks impossible. If you think about it, it is impossible. If you take the jump it is possible. So for those who go on thinking about it, it becomes more and more impossible. The more you think, the more impossible it appears. It is for the courageous ones to take the jump.

It is said, "Think twice before you jump." I say, "First jump, and then think as much as you want!" Twice or thrice...as much as you want. Be at ease, think to your heart's content – but take the jump first!

CONTEMPLATION BEFORE SLEEP

Meditation leads you towards the oceanic – from smallness to vastness, from the bounded body-mind structure to the unbounded consciousness, from the finite to the infinite, from time to eternity, from birth and death to eternal life.

The only requirement is to drop the notion of the ego, and it is not difficult for the intelligent person to do. The more intelligent one is, the more easily he can drop the idea, because he can see that it is an absolutely wrong notion.

We cannot be separate – we cannot exist even for a single moment in separation. If the breath does not go in, we are gone. We are continuously exchanging. Breathing means the bridge between us and the whole. The breath is something like roots in the whole: you pull the tree out of the earth and it starts dying. It loses its roots; they were its nourishment. Stop breathing and one dies.

Breathing is a subtle way of our being rooted in the whole. The very word 'breath' means life, because without breath there is no life. That is the only indication whether a man is alive or not. If he is breathing he is alive, if he is not breathing he is dead. But because the breath is not visible, we don't take any account of it. Otherwise we are continuously taking something from existence each moment.

So if we look into life we can be very easily aware that ego is a false idea. And the moment you drop the ego, all barriers are dropped – you rush into the ocean, you become one with the ocean. The experience is the ultimate experience of ecstasy, of freedom.

d a y

27

Meditation is the art of landing you at your very centre.

We live on the circumference – how to jump from the circumference to the centre? It is a whole art. I call it art rather than science because science is more mathematical and art is more artistic, more poetic.

In science there are no exceptions, it follows universal laws. In art there are exceptions; in fact every individual reaches his centre in a slightly different way from anybody else, because each individual has something unique in him. That is the divinity and the great grace of the universe – that it makes unique individuals only.

Meditation is the bridge between the circumference and the centre, between the outer and the inner, between mind and no-mind, between matter and consciousness.

CONTEMPLATION BEFORE SLEEP

Meditation is the greatest miracle there is. It is the greatest gift that has been given by the awakened ones to humanity. Science has given many things, but nothing compared to meditation. And one cannot conceive that science will ever be able to give anything comparable to meditation. Up to now meditation has been the greatest gift to humanity, and it is going to remain the greatest gift forever. That can be safely predicted for the simple reason that science goes on studying the objective world; meditation gives you mastery of your subjective existence, your inner world – and the inner is always higher than the outer. Science cannot be greater than the scientist, obviously: the object cannot be higher, more valuable than the observer.

It is the fear of the unknown that keeps us clinging to all kinds of suffering. The suffering is not clinging to you, you cling to it. People prefer suffering more to nothingness. Nothingness is not only better than suffering, it is better than everything, it is better than the whole. To be nothing, to be a nobody, to be an utter nonentity certainly needs guts. It is moving to the farthest shore without knowing whether it exists or not. It is losing this shore, which has become very well-known, and taking a quantum leap towards something which may be, may not be – there is no guarantee.

That's why a master is needed. A master is not a guarantee of the unknown, for the unknown, but a witness. He cannot guarantee truth for you. He can only share: "It is – I have known it, I am a witness to it." And if, looking into his eyes, you can feel the trust, if you can feel his love and your love for him, then something starts transpiring, then something mysterious starts happening. That mysterious relationship is disciplehood, that is sannyas. It is the most mysterious experience of life. Even the experience of love is nothing compared to it.

CONTEMPLATION BEFORE SLEEP

Man can live in two ways. He can live a life which is enclosed from all sides, encapsulated. There are reasons why millions of people choose this kind of life – it is safe, secure, cosy, but they are missing something far more valuable because they will miss adventure and they will miss the exploration of the truth and they will miss godliness and they will miss love, they will miss light. In fact they will miss all and what they will get is just a comfortable death. Their life is the life of the grave. Of course in a grave there is no danger, you cannot die again. It is the safest place, but even though it is safe you have lost life.

Godliness is possible only when one learns to live the second kind of life. The first is encapsulated. That is the choice of millions. That's why they are just walking graves – alive only in the animal sense of being alive, in fact vegetating. They don't have souls.

When one starts living dangerously one lives for the first time. And to live dangerously is to live a divine life. Jesus lived dangerously, Buddha lived dangerously, Socrates lived dangerously, Al-Hillaj Mansoor lived dangerously. But these were the people who reached the highest peak of being individuals. They came to know the Everest of consciousness.

day
31

God has no form, no name, no definition.
God is indefinable, indescribable, inexpressible. Hence whatsoever has been said about God is all wrong. The moment it is said, it becomes wrong.

One can be right about God only if one remains silent. Utter a single word and you have missed the point. Nothing can be said about God, but God can be an experience. There is no proof, no logical certainty, but there is something existential.

Sannyas is a new way of looking at things. It is a method of looking at things so that slowly slowly God starts emerging from everywhere. Although he has no form, he starts expressing himself in all forms possible. You start feeling him in all forms.

In one sense one wave is the ocean; in another sense every wave is the ocean. In one sense no form is God; in another sense every form is divine.

Mind cannot know because mind can only catch hold of forms. To know the formless you will have to go beyond the mind, you will have to drop the mind at least for a few moments every day, so that you can be bathed with God. And those few moments are the real moments. These are the only moments that you have lived; all other moments will go down the drain, they will not be saved – only those moments that you have lived with God, with the presence of God are saved.

MONTH 4

Meditation is fire

Flow with the river, go with the river, abandon yourself totally to the river. It is already going to the ocean, it will take you to the ocean too; you need not even swim.

The ocean represents existence, and unless we find the ocean we cannot be contented – because of the limitations, boundaries. All boundaries are bondages. The moment the river falls into the ocean it becomes infinite, it becomes eternal. And that is the goal of sannyas: to help you reach the infinite, the eternal, the vast, the unlimited, the indefinable, the ineffable.

d
a
y
2

Life means remaining always flowing, moving. Go on reaching for the farthest star. Enjoy the very journey – don't be too worried about the goals. Goals are only excuses so that one can go on and on in the journey. In fact, there are no goals in life. Life is a pilgrimage, a pilgrimage to nothing, a pilgrimage to nowhere – just a pure pilgrimage.

To understand this brings great freedom, brings great unburdening. All anxieties, all anguishes drop; all worries disappear, evaporate, because when there is no goal you cannot fail. Failure is our idea because we believe in a goal.

For example, I can never fail because I have no goal. I can never feel frustrated because I never expect anything. If something happens, good; if nothing happens, far out! Either way it is always good.

And that is my fundamental teaching: Live each moment in its totality. It is not a means to some end. But in the beginning it is very difficult so I go on giving you false goals and aims. They are just toys; you can go on without them. Once you start enjoying the journey itself then there is no reason for any goal. Then you don't ask for the meaning of life, life is its own meaning; it is an end unto itself.

And this is the state of total freedom.

CONTEMPLATION BEFORE SLEEP

Freedom is one of the most significant qualities. In fact, it is out of freedom that all that is great blooms. You can love only if you are free. You can seek truth only if you are free. You can be joyous only if you are free. Hence freedom has to become the very foundation of sannyas.

I don't want you to belong to the church, to a creed, to a nation, to a race. Those are all ugly things. One should be free of all that nonsense. One should be simply human. There is no need to be a Christian, or Hindu or Mohammedan, and no need to be Indian, an American or a German. One should be free of all these bondages. These are prisons which keep your spirit encaged. Break out!

And it is all up to you. If you cooperate with all these things you are cooperating with your slavery. Stop cooperating. Nobody else is keeping you in bondage, it is your own unawareness. So become aware of how you cooperate with your slavery, and that very awareness is enough to get rid of all slavery.

Freedom is your nature. It is not to be achieved. When all slavery disappears one is free, when the slavery is no longer present freedom starts welling up within your being. And out of freedom life starts taking on tremendous beauty. Then everything is possible – love, truth, godliness.

day **4**

We are seeds but it would be unfortunate to die as a seed. We have to become flowers and we have to release our fragrance; only then is there contentment. A tree is fulfilled when it blooms, when the spring comes and the tree has released, poured its heart into colours, into fragrance, into joy. When the tree is dancing in the wind, in the sun, it is fulfilled.

My work here is to make you aware of your great potential, of your infinite possibility, of the heights that you can reach, of the depths that you can penetrate. Your heights are higher than the Himalayas, and your depths are deeper than the Pacific. And once you know your heights and your depths, life becomes nothing but gratitude. Existence has given you so much. It has poured all its creativity into your being, it has made you so rich, so inexhaustibly rich...and we are living like beggars.

My sannyas means a declaration that you are no more a beggar, but an emperor, an empress.

CONTEMPLATION BEFORE SLEEP

As you live more experiences, more memories accumulate, and it becomes a mountain – really heavy. People are crushed under it. The moment you see that it is useless you can drop it. It is not clinging to you, you are clinging to it, so you simply take your hands away.

Then the next thing that comes through watchfulness is that you become aware that the future is not yet, so why be bothered about it? When it comes we will see, we will respond. There is no need to be worried about it – it may never come or it may come in such a way that you cannot imagine it right now. It is unpredictable. Whatsoever you think about it, ninety-nine per cent of it is never going to happen. And wasting your energy for that one per cent is sheer foolishness.

Once you see it you withdraw from the future – and the past and the future are one hundred per cent of your mind, the whole content. Fifty per cent belongs to the past and fifty per cent to the future. In the present there is no content. If one is just here now then consciousness is empty.

You can see, whenever you look in your mind either something from the past is moving or something from the future. As far as this very moment is concerned consciousness is pure. And the meditator, by slowly slowly dropping the past and the future, starts settling in the present.

To live here and now is to live a religious life. That is pure consciousness, and out of pure consciousness whatsoever happens is virtue. Whatsoever you do is right. Whatever your response you will never repent it, you will never feel guilty for it.

d
a
y

6

Anything that has a boundary will imprison you. All boundaries have to be transcended, surpassed.

When you have come to a point where no boundary to your being exists, when you are simply without any definition, when you have transcended all boundaries of the body and the mind, you enter an oceanic world.

So there is no need to cling, no need to become attached to anything. Remain unattached so that your flow is not hindered. Remain like a river. It passes through many territories, through many beautiful valleys, mountains, forests, but it goes on moving. It passes through many beautiful scenes but without clinging; it goes on and on till it reaches the ocean.

Be like a river, flowing, never getting attached; otherwise you will become a pond. And a pond can never reach the ocean, only a river can. So remain open-ended and go on flowing. Then the ocean is not far away. However far away it is, it is not far away.

CONTEMPLATION BEFORE SLEEP

My effort is to help you to accept yourself as you are and to go on searching and seeking for your authentic soul.

It is burdened with so many stupid ideas that you will have to unburden yourself, empty yourself. Only by emptying all the nonsense that has been given to you by others will you be able to have the first contact, the first connection with your being.

It is a tremendous freedom. It is freedom from time, freedom from mind, freedom from death. Suddenly you enter into the dimension of eternity; suddenly you become contemporaries of God. Less than that is not worthwhile.

d
a
y
8

Deep down in the heart it has to be understood that life is a gift of tremendous value, that each moment is precious, that it has not to be wasted. It is a great opportunity to grow. One should not go on collecting coloured stones and seashells on the sea beach. Something more important has to be done, something more significant.

One has to look inwards. One should not remain concerned just about outside things, because that's how people waste their lives. One should start searching within. One should go deeper and deeper into one's consciousness to feel one's centre. The moment that you feel your centre all questions are answered, all puzzles disappear. There is no confusion any more. Everything is a clarity, a transparent clarity. You can see through and through. And that is the moment when one understands how much the universe has given to us, and how ungrateful we have been to the universe.

Gratitude is the basic requirement for a religious life. It is out of gratitude that prayer arises, it is out of gratitude that love arises, it is out of gratitude that grace arises. But one can feel gratitude only if one feels the value, the immense value of life, the inestimable value of existence.

CONTEMPLATION BEFORE SLEEP

Once you are awakened you start living life in a totally different way. Although your life remains the same you are no more the same. Your approach is different, your very style is different. You live more consciously. You don't go on groping in darkness. You live through the heart and not through the head. Your life becomes love, compassion. It becomes a song, a dance, a celebration. And of course whosoever comes in contact with you will be infected by it. It is contagious. It is like fire, wildfire; it goes on spreading.

day
10

God is unbounded, infinite, vast. God is oceanic and we are like dewdrops. We have to learn the art of disappearing into the ocean. It needs guts, because to disappear into the ocean means to die as a dewdrop, because unless one dies as a dewdrop one cannot be born as the ocean. When the seed dies as a seed a great tree is born. The seed disappears; only through its disappearance does the tree appear.

CONTEMPLATION BEFORE SLEEP

For God there is no darkness. For light there is no darkness.

Darkness exists only when light is absent; hence they never meet. Light does not know that darkness exists at all. How can light know? – because when light is present, darkness is not. Darkness is only an absence. God knows no darkness. And we know only darkness – that's how we have been unbridged with God.

We also have to reach a point where darkness disappears and only light remains. That day, when darkness disappears for you, is of great celebration, is a day of great blessing. It is possible only when you realize that you are light.

d a y

12

Become blissful, become luminous. The flame is already there. You do not have to do anything, you just have to discover it. It is within you so you do not have to go anywhere else. Just be in silence, be still, looking in, searching.

You will have to pass through a big crowd of thoughts and desires, but it is not as big as it appears from the outside. Yes, you have to push and pull a little bit and you have to force yourself inwards a little bit. But it is a beautiful game, it is fun! To meditate is fun. And once you have been able to pass through the crowd into the open space of your inner being you will see the flame. That's your inner being. That flame is part of the great flame of existence, part of the universal fire.

CONTEMPLATION BEFORE SLEEP

Man is an unopened scripture.
We go on reading the vedas, the bibles, the korans, but we never read our inner being. And all that is contained in the vedas, in the bibles, in the korans, is contained within you, and is contained within you in absolute purity. Vedas are contaminated; bibles, korans are contaminated. It is the nature of things: the moment you speak a truth it becomes a lie, utter it and you have already made it false. It remains true only when it lives in deep silence within you.

It is only within your own being that you will find the still, small voice of God. Just one condition has to be fulfilled: you have to become silent, noiseless, so that you can hear it, so that you can read it.

day 14

In your true reality you are a God. You may have fallen asleep and you may be dreaming that you have become a beggar, that you are a man or a woman, that you are white or black, that you are this or that, that you are poor or rich – but all those are just dreams. When the mind stops dreaming only one thing remains, and that is, "I am God."

To die without knowing this is to have lived in a futile way. One is fulfilled only when one knows, "I am God." And it is not a question of believing. The priests have been saying for centuries that the kingdom of God is within you – but that doesn't help. You need to experience it on your own.

Belief is easy; you can start believing that you are a God. That will simply be megalomania, that will simply be madness. It is a question of experiencing.

When you believe that you are a God, when you believe that, "I am God," the 'I' is very important and God is just a shadow. When you experience, "I am God," the 'I' is just a word, a utilitarian word; only the God is real. That's the difference between the madman and the mystic. The madman can also declare, "I am God," but he is simply declaring, "I am." And this is the ultimate ego, to declare that, "I am God." The mystic also declares, "I am God," but he says, "I am not; hence I am God."

So I am not telling you to believe it. I am saying that you have to experience it. Don't leave this life without experiencing it. This is an opportunity to experience your reality.

CONTEMPLATION BEFORE SLEEP

Unless one realizes one's godhood nothing is achieved, life has been a failure. And one can realize it, it is every man's birthright; but one has to claim it, one has to work for it, one has to be very creative about it, using every possibility to grow: to grow beyond humanity, to surpass humanity, to become divine – because that is our reality.

Man is not as small as he appears. He is vast, he is tremendously vast. He is oceanic. Even the ocean has boundaries, and man has no boundaries. Even the ocean is not so vast. Man's vastness is the only proof that God is. God is another name for man's vastness. We are not confined to the body and we are not confined to the mind either. We are beyond both.

The whole process of sannyas is that of peeling an onion. There are many layers of identification, and we have to drop all the layers, slowly, slowly, slowly. Finally nothing is left – that nothing is you.

Only nothing can be vast. Something is bound to be finite. Only nothing is infinite; hence God is ultimate nothingness. God is not a being but the ultimate non-being. He is not somebody, he is absolutely nobodiness. He is only a presence, infinite, unbounded. And so are we. We are not different from God. We are part of that infinity.

*d
a
y*

17

All that is valuable has harmony in it as its very core. Without harmony there is no God. The harmony in existence proves that something keeps it together, something invisible. Without harmony there is no love. But it is an invisible thread, nobody can see it.

Everybody can feel it. Love makes one aware of the fact that all that is seen may not be all, there may be more than you can see. Reality is not finished with seeing. There is a different plane of feeling too which is far deeper, far more basic.

Without harmony there is no joy. When you are in harmony cheerfulness radiates from you naturally, spontaneously. It becomes your vibe.

A harmonious person is bound to be cheerful and bound to be beautiful. That is inevitable, because there is nothing more beautiful than cheerfulness, there is nothing more graceful than harmony.

day 18

Love is nothing but the disappearance of the dewdrop in the ocean. It is losing one's ego, it is total surrender to existence. It is meeting with the whole, it is dropping your boundaries and your identity. It is abandoning yourself. The moment you abandon yourself, immediately you become oceanic, vast.

We are clinging to our identity. We protect it, we fight for it, we are even ready to die for it. And this is just stupidity because the ego is the most false thing in existence. It is just hot air, it has no real existence. It is like darkness.

You can see darkness, every day you see it, but it has no existence as such. It is simply absence of light – nothing in itself, just an absence of light. Bring the light in and you don't find any darkness, and you never even see it going out of the door. Turn the light out and it is suddenly there. It does not come in; you can keep the doors and windows closed. It comes from nowhere because it is non-existential, it is just absence. It does not come and go. Light comes and goes because light is.

The same is true about your ego. Ego is absence of love. The moment you bring the light of love in, ego disappears. You need not do anything else for the ego; just become more loving, unconditionally loving.

CONTEMPLATION BEFORE SLEEP

Love is not addressed to anybody in particular; just be loving – that has to be your quality. It has nothing to do with relationship. Love has to be like fragrance. Whether anybody comes to know it or not, does not matter to the flower. Even in the farthest Himalayas, where nobody comes and goes, thousands of flowers bloom and spread their fragrances.

In the Himalayas there is a whole valley of very strange flowers. People have only seen the valley from the peaks, nobody has been able to reach it because to go down into the valley is dangerous. People know about those flowers but nobody has smelled their perfume; and they have very psychedelic colours. They are far away, but they are not worried at all about that; the flowers are perfectly happy.

Love has to be your quality. Become loving, and one day it happens that you are simply love; not even loving but love. That is the day of great revelation. In that very moment the dewdrop disappears into the ocean and becomes the ocean.

d
a
y

20

This is the whole secret on the path of love: unmotivated love transforms your whole being into love energy, and to become love energy is to become divine. Nothing more is needed. That is more than one can ask for, that is more than one can dream of. It brings absolute fulfilment, it brings flowering. You bloom. Flowers of consciousness start opening within you.

CONTEMPLATION BEFORE SLEEP

Meditation only takes you up to the door. But that is the greatest journey – from the head to the heart, from logic to love, from knowing to feeling. Hence the poet is closer than the scientist, the dancer is closer than the politician, the lover is closer than the businessman. But it is only through meditation that the poet will become aware of that one step; otherwise one can stand at the door of the temple keeping the door behind one.

That's how the poet is standing: standing at the door of the temple but looking out. The mystic is also standing at the same door, but looking in. They are standing on the same spot; the thing that makes the difference is meditation. Meditation gives you a one-hundred-and-eighty-degree turn; you don't look outside, you look in.

The directions of the poet and mystic are different. They are located in the same space, on the same step; the poet and the mystic are exactly on the same step, standing at the same door. But the poet is looking outside and the mystic is looking inside – and that makes the difference, the greatest difference.

The moment the mystic looks in, he rushes in. Then he cannot stop, nothing can stop him. The urge to rush in is irresistible.

Meditation makes you capable of the ultimate step. So focus your whole effort, your whole being on only one thing, keep one word constantly in remembrance – meditation – and put your total energy into it so that it can become a reality for you.

To enter into meditation, one of the most essential qualities is patience. One cannot be in a hurry. The more in a hurry one is, the longer it takes. If one is capable of waiting forever – lovingly, trustingly – it can happen even in a single moment. Instantly it can happen, immediately it can happen; it all depends on how patient one is.

But remember, while doing meditation never bother about the result. It will come in its own time. Trust! Enjoy meditation for its own sake, don't be greedy about it, don't project any ambition. If one can do meditation not as a means but as an end unto itself, then the miracle can happen immediately, it can change your total being.

The transformation is easy. One has to learn the art of being patient – which humanity has completely forgotten. Everybody is in such a hurry, everybody wants things to happen quickly. Nobody is ready to wait. That's why there are so many charlatans in the world of religion. You ask for instant coffee so there are pedlars who sell instant coffee, and they exploit you.

My approach is of patience, infinite patience – and then the miracle is that it can happen even like instant coffee. But the requirement has to be fulfilled. It is a paradox, but anything concerned with the truth is always paradoxical; it has to be paradoxical, because truth needs to be inclusive of its opposite.

CONTEMPLATION BEFORE SLEEP

One has to be very playful about meditation, one has to learn to enjoy it as fun. One has not to be serious about it – be serious and you miss. One has to go into it very joyfully.

And one has to keep aware that it is falling into deeper and deeper rest. It is not concentration, just the contrary: it is relaxation. When you are utterly relaxed, for the first time you start feeling your reality, you come face to face with your being. When you are engaged in activity you are so occupied that you cannot see yourself. Activity creates much smoke around you, it raises much dust around you; hence all activity has to be dropped, at least for a few hours a day.

That is only so in the beginning. When you have learned the art of being at rest, then you can be both active and restful together, because then you know that rest is something so inner that it cannot be disturbed by anything outer: the activity goes on at the circumference and at the centre you remain restful. So it is only for beginners that activity has to be dropped for a few hours. When one has learned the art, then there is no question: for twenty-four hours a day one can be meditative and one can continue all the activities of ordinary life.

day
24

Meditation does two things to you: one, it makes you aware of the beauty that exists all around, it makes you sensitive to it; and the second thing, it makes you beautiful, it gives you a certain grace. Your eyes become full of beauty because the whole existence is beautiful, we just have to drink out of it, we just have to allow the beauty to enter us.

Ordinarily a person is not aware of the beauty that surrounds existence. He is more aware of all that is ugly because the mind always goes on finding the negative. It counts the thorns, it misses the roses. It counts the wounds, it misses the blessings. That's the way of the mind.

The moment you move into meditation, the moment you become a little more silent, a little more calm and quiet, more relaxed, more rested in your being, you suddenly become aware of the beauty of the trees, of the beauty of the clouds, the beauty of people, of everything that is there.

Everything is beautiful because it is full of godliness; even rocks are overflowing with godliness. Nothing is empty of godliness. And once you start experiencing all these beautiful dimensions the ultimate result is that nourished by your beautiful experience – by music, by poetry, by dance, by celebration, by love – you become beautiful. A natural outcome is that a grace arises in your being. It starts radiating. Everybody can see it, unless one is determined not to; that is another matter. If one wants to see it, it is there. But people who are determined to remain with closed eyes, of course, cannot see it.

CONTEMPLATION BEFORE SLEEP

Roses are beautiful, lotuses are beautiful, but they are not flowers of beauty. They are beautiful flowers, of course, but not flowers of beauty. Flowers of beauty happen in your innermost core. They happen through inner growth, when you transform your potential into actuality. When you really become a being, when there is no more to life, when you have experienced life in its totality, then something flowers in you. That flowering brings you for the first time a gift from existence.

There are many gifts from existence – birth is a gift, life is a gift, love is a gift – but the ultimate gift is when your consciousness becomes a lotus. When one flower of beauty blooms in you. In Japan they call it satori, in India we call it samadhi. It can be translated as ultimate ecstasy.

The lotus symbolizes the ultimate flowering of consciousness. Right now you are just like a bud, closed; hence your fragrance is not being released. Sannyas is the process of opening the petals of the lotus. Sannyas is like sunrise. Being with a master means entering into a sunlit world. And as the sun rises the lotus petals start opening, naturally – they are not to be forced – and then great fragrance is released. That fragrance is bliss, peace, celebration. One has come to fulfilment, one has come to be utterly contented because one has given whatsoever was one's destiny, and has poured it into existence. Whatsoever one was capable of contributing, creating, one has done it. That is the ultimate act of creativity, and naturally after that ultimate act one feels utterly satisfied, contented.

d
a
y

27

Love yourself because it is only through love that you will become harmonious, that you will become one. Don't condemn yourself. You have been given a beautiful body. You have been given a beautiful mechanism called mind. If you use it rightly it is of tremendous importance; if it becomes the master then it is dangerous. If you remain the master then there is no problem, it is a beautiful servant. And you have been given a soul – a piece of existence. One cannot ask for more.

Light is possible, but only through love. Without love only darkness is possible. In the inner world love and light are synonymous; they don't mean different things. Hence one who wants to be full of light, one who wants to be enlightened, has to be unconditionally loving.

Love without any demands. Demands make it ugly, demands destroy it. If you have some conditions attached to your love, it remains no more love, it becomes lust. And it becomes a political game, a power trip.

Let your love remain pure and let your love remain unconfined; don't make any boundaries to it. Let it remain unaddressed, so slowly slowly it is not a question of whom to love, what to love; the only question is how to be loving. The object of love is irrelevant.

Just as the body needs breath – it is its life – the soul needs love – it is the nourishment for your soul. The more you love, the more soul you have. When your love is infinite your soul also has infinity. When your love knows no bounds your being also knows no bounds. That's what is really meant by God-realization: it is love-realization and nothing else.

d
a
y

29

L ove is the surest way to real victory, but it is a very strange way, very paradoxical, because love begins in surrender and ends in victory. That's its paradox: love does not want to be victorious but it becomes victorious. Love wants to surrender, but surrender brings victory.

And the people who try to be victorious remain failures. They may become victorious in the eyes of the world but that is not true victory because death will take it away. True victory is that which even death cannot destroy.

Think of yourself as victorious only when you have gained something of immortality. Love gives you the first glimpse of immortality, love opens the first window beyond death. One who knows love is bound to know existence sooner or later, one just has to go on deepening one's love. Be in love with love itself, then victory is going to be yours.

d
a
y
30

Be blissful within and loving without. One can be blissful and miserly – then bliss starts dying. It has to be shared to keep it alive and flowing, to keep it fresh and young.

The old tradition of the so-called religious people has been very miserly; there was no place for love in it. Of course they were all searching for bliss and they could find little bits of blissfulness here and there, but they were very greedy and miserly. And in their greed and miserliness whatsoever they found was killed, destroyed, poisoned; hence they remained sad. All the saints look sad, they have long faces – with no laughter, with no love, with no sharing.

This is something very fundamental, that bliss grows as you share it, otherwise it dies. Even if by chance you discover a source of it, soon it will be exhausted. If you want it to be inexhaustible, then share, then share as much as possible. And never think whether the other person is worthy or not. Those are the considerations of a greedy person, a miserly person.

A person who wants to share never thinks whether the other is worthy or not. Who cares? The whole point is to share. If he is ready to share, that's enough. Be thankful that he allows you to share your joy.

The sharing of bliss is love, and it is through love that bliss grows. The more you love, the more blissful you become; the more blissful you become the more you love. They feed each other. And between the two you become an integrated being.

CONTEMPLATION BEFORE SLEEP

The mind is a wall, meditation is a bridge. The mind disconnects, meditation reconnects. And once you are one with the whole that means you are one with the trees and the mountains and the rivers and the stars and the sun and the moon. Then this infinity is yours and all its joys are yours. Life starts having freedom for the first time because all limitations disappear – and that is the ultimate desire of the human heart.

We are searching continuously for the union; knowingly or unknowingly we want to merge with the whole, because only with the whole does life come to its ultimate peak, does ecstasy attain its Everest.

MONTH 5

Play with life

Unless existence dances in you there is no possibility of any dance. Unless existence rejoices in you there is no possibility of rejoicing.

Remove yourself so that you don't come in between you and existence. Put the ego, the very idea of 'I', aside and be utterly empty, receptive. And the moment your emptiness is total, the whole starts showering millions of joys and millions of flowers upon you. The splendour is infinite.

C onsecrated to God' is exactly the definition of sannyas.

One starts living not for the ego but for the whole, one starts living as a vehicle of God, one becomes just like a hollow bamboo so that God can transform one into a flute. One empties oneself of oneself.

That's all that needs to be done: one has to empty oneself of oneself. And when one is empty something mysterious starts happening, unexplainable. Something of the beyond starts descending in you, some unknown force starts singing through you, dancing through you.

That unknown force is God. God is not a person; it is only a name for all that is mysterious, for all that is beyond comprehension, for all that intellect is incapable of understanding. And to be consecrated to the miraculous, to the mysterious, is the only way to live a beautiful, graceful life. Otherwise people are only dragging themselves along. Their life is not a dance, it cannot be.

d
a
y
3

All that is great is always a gift of existence. It is never our achievement; in fact it happens only when we are utterly absent. Love happens when you are absent, truth happens when you are absent, bliss happens when you are absent. When you are too full of yourself nothing happens. Then gifts go on coming but you are not ready to receive them. The ego is very non-receptive. We can receive existence's gifts only when we are utterly empty; the emptier you are the better.

Existence is not miserly. It gives, and it gives much. It is willing to give everything, but we are not ready to receive. We don't have any space to receive its gifts.

So start emptying yourself and you will be moving in the right direction.

CONTEMPLATION BEFORE SLEEP

The God of meditation is the only true God. All other gods are inventions – inventions of crafty priests, inventions of greedy minds, inventions out of fear. The only true God, which is not an invention, is experienced through meditation, because meditation requires you first to drop all thoughts, including thoughts about God.

When all thoughts and desires have been dropped, then whatsoever you have come to know is not part of your mind because we have put the mind aside from the very beginning. Now there is nobody to invent anything. Now you will know that which is.

day
5

Man tries in every possible way to achieve bliss, by accumulating money, by becoming powerful, by becoming respectable, by becoming knowledgeable. But all these ways are doomed to fail. They cannot bring bliss to you. Bliss comes only in one way and that is by your becoming more conscious. The more you are conscious, the more you are blissful; the less conscious, the more miserable.

As consciousness becomes bigger and unconsciousness shrinks, you become blissful, more and more blissful. You start opening up like a flower. We are like buds, closed; as bliss comes you become a flower. In the East we say that one becomes a lotus, a one-thousand-petalled lotus. Everybody is carrying the seed, the bud, but great effort is needed to be conscious. Unconsciousness has been our habit for so many lives that it has almost become our nature.

So from this moment try to be more and more conscious, in everything that you do, in everything that you think, in everything that you feel. These are the three dimensions. In all these three dimensions you have to become more watchful, more alert, more of a witness. Between these three arises the fourth, the witness – and that is your true nature.

Once you have learned how to create the witness you know the secret art, you know the alchemy of transforming the dark continent in your being into light.

CONTEMPLATION BEFORE SLEEP

When you do something creative a great contentment arises. When you finish a painting, a silence falls over you. You feel fulfilled, meaningful, significant, you have done something. You have participated in God's work. He is a creator and you have been a creator in your own way, a small way of course, but you have participated with God, you walked with God – maybe only a few steps, but you walked with God.

But the ultimate act of creativity is the flowering of your consciousness. After that you never leave God for a single moment. Then the whole pilgrimage is with him, within him. Naturally it is tremendously fulfilling. There can be no other fulfilment higher than that, greater than that. It is the very peak.

day 7

People go on doing a thousand other things rather than coming back home. If they are miserable they go on throwing responsibility onto others. The wife is creating the trouble, the husband thinks that's why he is miserable...or the society or the state. There are a thousand and one excuses. One can always find them, they are always available. If you can't find them you can invent them. But no excuse is going to help, it simply prolongs your misery more. There is no excuse for your misery except the truth – and the truth is that you are very far away from your being.

So whenever you are miserable go into meditation: become silent, watch your misery; become a witness to it, don't become identified with it, and you will be surprised that the more you watch, the less it is. And when you are perfectly watchful it simply disappears, as if it has never been there. Not even a trace is left behind. And suddenly you will find that the same energy that was becoming your misery has become a showering of bliss. You have come home.

CONTEMPLATION BEFORE SLEEP

Life is something tremendously beautiful but we are unaware of it, we are blind to it. It is glory, but we are not sensitive enough to receive it.

Life is perfect but our sensitivity is almost nil; hence the whole problem is how to create more sensitivity, how to become more alive, how to be more open, vulnerable, so that one can feel the life that surrounds us. The moment we are in step with life, life is God, and there is no other God.

And life knows no death, no birth. It is eternal, and we are part of that eternity. But we have gathered much rust around our mirrorlike being so that it reflects nothing. Our mind is like a layer of dust on our consciousness; hence nothing is reflected and we cannot see that which is. We only see the dust; we only see our thoughts, our desires, our memories, our dreams – and they are not the reality. Unless all this dust is cleaned away we will not be able to reflect that which is.

As one becomes more and more silent, peaceful, alert, sensitive, life becomes more glorious, more beautiful, more blissful. It is a great gift. But we are wasting time and opportunity, we are not appreciating that which has been given to us. We don't deserve it.

day **9**

We are all strangers on this earth. Our real home is on the other shore.

We are here only to be ready to grow, to experience, to mature, so that we can be accepted on the other shore. We come into this life just as children are sent to school. It is a learning place, it is not our home. Learn as much as you can, experience as deeply as possible. Let your life be multi-dimensional, but remember one thing, that this is not our home. So don't get attached, don't become possessive, don't start clinging; otherwise who will go to the other shore?

When the evening comes the child returns to his home. For the whole day he is in the school, in the evening he comes back. The school is a necessity; without it he cannot grow. With all its pleasures and pains, with all its foolishness and wisdoms, with all the joys and miseries we slowly slowly learn balancing, centring. Passing through many many agonies and ecstasies, something inside us matures, integrates. And when we are ready the boat arrives from the other shore to take us back home, but only when we are ready. Otherwise we are sent again and again, until we learn the lesson.

CONTEMPLATION BEFORE SLEEP

I have heard a story of a great musician. He was singing a song, and the people who were listening to him were great lovers of music. He finished one song and the whole crowd said, "Again, once more." He sang it again, very happy that he had been received so well. When he finished it the whole crowd shouted even more loudly, "Again, once more!" He sang it again.

When he finished for the third time the crowd shouted even louder. Then he said, "But I can sing other songs too."

Then one person in the crowd said, "Until you sing it right, we are going to say, 'Again, again, again."

That's what happens in life: we are sent again, again and again. You can die, but you will be sent back until you have learned the lesson. And the lesson *can* be learned.

There are only two types of people in the world, those who complain and those who praise. The complainers remain miserable because their heart never opens up, never becomes a flower. Their very approach is negative. They only look at the darker side of things, they never look at the brighter side. They count thorns, they never praise the roses.

When you start praising the beauty of the flowers and the silence of darkness and the joy of the river rushing towards the ocean, something starts opening up within you. You also start growing, you are no longer closed. The praise becomes a bridge between you and existence. You become more and more sensitive, more and more poetic, more and more aesthetic. Your sensibility makes you aware of the immense beauty that surrounds us, and of the great mystery which is unfathomable, which has no beginning and no end.

The feeling that we are a part of this great mystery creates great rejoicing. Praise is prayer, and bliss is the fragrance of prayer.

CONTEMPLATION BEFORE SLEEP

Without contributing to life nobody can ever feel blissful. So many people search for bliss but they fail for the simple reason that they are uncreative. They don't create anything.

There is one joy and only one joy in the world, and that is of creating something, whatsoever that is: a poem, a song, a little music...whatsoever it is. But unless you create something you will not feel fulfilled. Only by creating something do you participate in God's being. God is the creator of the whole, and when you create a small thing, in a small way you become part of God. That's the only way to bridge the gap between you and God. No other prayer is going to help, no ritual is of any significance. They are just deceptive strategies invented by clever and cunning priests.

The real prayer is to be creative. But how can you create if you don't know what your potential is, if you don't know in what direction you have to move so that you can become creative and can attain fulfilment?

The work of meditation is simply to make you aware of your own potential. It simply throws light inside you, it focuses light on your inner being so that you can read the message.

d
a
y

13

Man is carrying within himself a tremendous capacity for music. When I say 'man' I mean every man, and when I say 'music' I don't mean ordinary music. Not everybody can be a musician in the ordinary sense. Only a few have that talent. It is something inborn, innate.

My meaning of music is totally different. I mean the inner experience of harmony. It is far more musical than any music that can be created. It is uncreated music. No instruments are needed, no training of expertise is needed. All that is required of you to listen to it, is a deep silence. It is already there. It is your very life. The Zen people call it the sound of one hand clapping.

In ordinary music there are always two things needed, only then can sound be created. If you are playing a guitar then you have to use your hands on the strings. Only through the tension created by your fingers will the strings create music. But the inner music is something which is already there from the very beginning. It is just like your heartbeat; a little deeper than that, a little more mysterious than the heartbeat. It is the beat of your true heart.

CONTEMPLATION BEFORE SLEEP

There have been two rivers of consciousness. One is of the philosophers – Aristotle in the West is the father of that, the originator. The other is of the mystics. That is a totally different kind of river. It has nothing to do with philosophizing, it is rooted in existential experience. And it has almost always happened that whenever there was a great mystic his followers always became divided between these currents.

The real ones, those who have understood the master, those who have really loved the master, became mystics. And those who have understood only the words of the master have become very knowledgeable; they became the philosophers.

Socrates was a mystic. Plato was his disciple but he lost track; he became a philosopher. Aristotle was Plato's disciple.

So from this very moment remember: my way is the way of the mystic, not of a philosopher. I believe in bliss, not in theories about bliss. And I want you to taste it, not just to think about it. It is pointless to go on thinking about food – it won't nourish you. It is stupid to go on thinking about water. Why? – when the river is flowing, you can drink and quench your thirst. There are foolish people who are standing or sitting on the bank and thinking about water, theorizing about water, finding what water consists of and dying of thirst!

So don't be a thinker, don't be a philosopher, be a mystic. My sannyasins have to be mystics, existential experiencers. It is a part of realization.

Life should be looked at not as prose but poetry. That's the religious approach, the approach of the mystic. He looks, not with questions in his eyes, he looks with wonder, he looks with awe. He does not think about existence, he feels it. He opens his heart; rather than using his head he throws the doors and windows of his heart open, he allows the sun and the wind and the rain to come in. That's what I mean by poetry.

The mystic is a poet in the ultimate sense. He may not write poetry – that is irrelevant – he lives poetry, he is poetry. Forget all about your head. Become headless and heart-full. There are no problems in life; all problems are fabrications of the mind. Life is a mystery to be lived, not a problem to be solved.

Live it, enjoy it, sing with it, dance with it, play with it! Don't try to be philosophical, be poetic, and all joy will be yours. And you will be able to attain the ultimate treasure, the kingdom of God. It is available only to the poets.

CONTEMPLATION BEFORE SLEEP

Everything that man has done to explain God has been destructive. Rather than making the world more religious, it has made the world less religious, because all these ideas are so inadequate that they can only satisfy fools. If you have a little intelligence then no religion can satisfy you. Just a little intelligence – not much! – then no religion can satisfy you. All religions have flaws, and such stupidities have been perpetuated. For example, the virgin birth of Jesus Christ.... That is a very essential thing, if you are to be a Christian. You have to believe in it. If you don't believe in it you are not a true Christian....

The real mystics have remained utterly silent about God, because the true God is known only in silence.

So drop all ideas of God and become more and more silent, and one day it is bound to happen: when the silence is total He comes so silently, so invisibly, that you are in for a great surprise. You don't hear His footsteps. One moment He was not there, the next moment He is there and you are overflowing with him. And you are no more the same person, and neither is the world the same.

day **17**

Man is powerful when he is with existence. Whenever he is not with existence he is absolutely powerless. Plugged into existence you have infinite power; unplugged you are just empty. And unfortunately millions of people are living their lives unplugged; hence so much misery, so much feeling of impotence, so much feeling of emptiness, so much feeling of futility.

Everybody once in a while finds life utterly absurd. There seems to be no sense in it. One goes on living because one is afraid to commit suicide, one is afraid of death – at least one is acquainted with this empty life. One never knows what is going to happen in death and after death, so it is better to go on dragging yourself along for the time being and hope for the best. But people are unplugged, that's the whole problem.

Religion simply means the art of getting plugged in to existence again. Then you are so full of power that it starts overflowing from you. You can share it and it is not exhausted. In fact the more you give it to others, the more you have it.

CONTEMPLATION BEFORE SLEEP

We live in desire. Desire means discontentment. Desire means that whatsoever is, is not right, not enough; more is needed. And desire is never fulfilled. It is unfillable by its very nature.

You can have as much as you desire, but the moment you have it desire goes on jumping ahead of you, it starts asking for more. Its greed knows no limits, it is unlimited greed. It is like the horizon: it looks so close – you can reach it within an hour if you run. But you can never reach it. The distance between you and the horizon will remain the same, constantly the same, because there is no horizon; it is an illusion. The earth is not meeting the sky anywhere, it only appears to be.

Such is the case with desire. It only appears that if I could reach that point, if I could attain to this or that, there would be contentment. I would be happy, I would be fulfilled. But it never happens.

One has to understand desiring and its futility. In that very understanding desire disappears and one is left at home in deep peace. When there is no desire, there is no disturbance. Desire is the only disturbance.

*d
a
y*
19

Our desires are dreams, all our thoughts are dreams. And we go on continuously living in dreams because we are asleep. Dreams can exist only if we are asleep, and dreams disappear the moment we awake. Going beyond dreams means awaking.

It is time. You have slept enough for many many lives. Don't miss this opportunity to wake up because rare is the opportunity, and to miss it is very easy. So put your whole energy into waking up.

In the beginning it seems almost impossible – how to do it? But if one goes on trying...in sleep one tosses and turns, but if one goes on tossing and turning, it is bound to disrupt the sleep. And just a moment's glimpse of being awake is enough to trigger a new process in your being. Then more and more moments of awakening happen.

And the day that one becomes fully awakened, twenty-four hours a day, even while one is asleep one remains alert, aware – when the body sleeps the soul never sleeps – when one is capable of being awake twenty-four hours a day even when the body is resting, then one should feel contented. One has arrived. Before that, make every possible effort that you can. Don't leave any stone unturned.

CONTEMPLATION BEFORE SLEEP

We are asleep, not in the ordinary sense but in a metaphysical sense. We don't know who we are, how can we be called awake? We don't know anything that is essential. We know much that is rubbish – we know everything about the moon and the sun and the earth and we know history and geography – but we know nothing about ourselves. We know nothing about the knower – and that should be the primary concern of any real education....

Fundamentally you have to become aware of yourself, of who you are. And only you can do that.

I can call you forth but you will have to come out, you will have to gather enough courage to come out of the darkness, out of the centuries-old habits, out of a long long sleep.

And when you are awake, life is a dance, a song, a bliss, a benediction.

d
a
y

21

To be a man is a great gift, but very few people realize it. You could have been anything in this vast universe – a rock, a cabbage, a potato...anything! And there is no court of appeal! Whatsoever one is, one is; nothing can be done about it. What can the poor potato do about it? But very few people realize that they are human beings and that they have tremendous potential to grow.

The beauty and the grandeur of being human is that it is only through being human that one can reach God. It is a first basic requirement. No other animal has any approach towards God, only man – and not even all men. Only people who are really alert and aware – those very few people create a bridge between themselves and God. Without that bridge life is meaningless and a great opportunity can be lost very easily.

CONTEMPLATION BEFORE SLEEP

There are many wrong ways towards God but only one right way. One wrong way is through fear. One will only think that one is moving, one will never move. That's why it is wrong. How can you go towards God if you are moving out of fear? The natural tendency when you are afraid is to escape. You can go away, farther away from God, but not closer to him. And all the religions have been teaching people to be afraid of God. Religious people are defined as God-fearing. Now, that is ridiculous – a religious person never fears God, he loves him.

Man can also move towards God through greed. That is the wrong way again, because greed means you want to exploit. Greed means you have certain desires to be fulfilled through God, God is not your goal. You want money, you want power, you want paradise, you want all the pleasures of paradise. And because that can be got only through God, out of compulsion you surrender to God. But God is the means, not the end, and to reduce God to a means is ugly, it is disgusting. God is the ultimate end, there is nothing beyond it.

And so on and so forth...these are the wrong ways. They appear to be ways but they are not ways they are walls. The only right way is love.

Love more, love deeply, love for love's sake, and you will be surprised that slowly slowly something new starts happening around you: the presence of God is felt.

d
a
y

23

Whenever you are in a loving space God fills it. And once you have tasted the joy of being filled with God you would like to remain in love twenty-four hours a day. Then love becomes your natural state and God becomes your inner experience. It is only through love that people have reached God. Others have been wandering astray.

Love is my message, but don't cling to the word 'love', don't make a gospel out of it. It is to be experienced.

CONTEMPLATION BEFORE SLEEP

A heart full of love, loyalty, trust is exactly the definition of a religious consciousness. These qualities are needed. Without these qualities one can never become aware of God, of love, of beauty, of the tremendous splendour of existence.

Existence is known through the heart, not through the head, and the heart approaches existence in deep love, trust. There is no other way to commune with the whole.

These qualities slowly slowly transform you. They transform you from doubting confusion into an absolute certainty of knowing. They take you out of the chaos of the head into the harmony of the heart. Remember them.

Prayer does not mean saying something to God, asking for something, prayer means listening to God. If you have to say something it can only be a thank you. A simple yes is enough.

But organized religions all over the world have been teaching people unnecessary prayers. And people are repeating those prayers, parrot-like. They have lost all meaning, they have become pure ritual, they are only formal.

You have to learn the true prayer. It consists of silence, it consists of deep listening. God wants to convey something to you. He is searching for you, but he never finds you because you are always so busy.

Be silent, more and more unoccupied, more and more available, and you will soon start hearing the still, small voice within. God does not speak from the outside, he speaks from your innermost core, he is already there. And to be connected with your innermost core is true prayer. The moment you are connected...it is so blissful, so ecstatic that you can only bow down in deep gratitude.

CONTEMPLATION BEFORE SLEEP

Worshippers are many, the world is full of them. Churches, mosques, temples, synagogues are all full of worshippers, but I don't call them worshippers. Their worship is only ritual. They are simply following a tradition. They are worshipping symbols. Their heart is not full of love, they don't really have a thirst for God; they are simply performing a social duty. Maybe they have become addicted to it, if they don't do it they feel something is missing....

I am not interested in rituals. I don't teach that you should say a particular prayer, that parrot-like you should repeat certain formulas in Arabic, in Hebrew, in Sanskrit – in some dead language, long-forgotten. I don't teach any gibberish. I simply teach you to love the beauty of existence that surrounds you. This is true worship because God is manifest; in thousands of ways he is available – in the trees, in the flowers, in the birds, in the mountains, in the sun, in the moon, in people, in animals. Feel him. Rather than believing, feel the beauty of existence, feel the splendour of the universe, the splendour of a night full of stars.

If a beautiful sunset cannot help you to pray, then no temple, no church, is going to help you. If a distant call of a cuckoo has no magic for you then you are dead, then worship cannot happen to you. Worship can happen only when the heart is throbbing with life.

d
a
y
27

Never be worried about what other people say about you, never take any note of it. Always think of only one thing: "God is my judge. Am I able to face God?" Let that be the criterion of your whole life and you will not go amiss.... One has to stand on one's own feet and the only consideration should be: Whatsoever I am doing should be according to my light. My consciousness should be the deciding factor. Then God is your judge.

CONTEMPLATION BEFORE SLEEP

Everyone is favoured by God equally. There is no partiality in existence. Existence is absolutely impartial. But that does not mean that it is cold. It is very warm, loving, protecting, caring. But we are not open to its warmth, we are closed.

The problem is with us, not with existence. Hence the whole effort down the ages has been a single one: to help people to open up so that they can commune with the stars and the clouds and the sun and the moon – because this totality is what God is. There is no God other than this existence. And unless you are open, fearlessly open, you will never become aware of what you are missing. You are missing life, you are missing love, you are missing truth.

Gather courage and open yourself to all the beauty and the blessing and the benediction. It is all yours. Just for the asking it is yours.

d a y

29

Priests down the ages have condemned man so much that everybody feels rejected, everybody feels, "I am just junk." Slowly slowly the priests have destroyed all self-respect. They have created a division in every person: the condemned part and the condemner.

The condemner they call your conscience and the condemned part they call your instincts. This division keeps you in a constant quarrel with yourself, in disharmony. You are at daggers with yourself, and that is no way to know existence.

The first lesson is to love yourself as you are, because existence loves you as you are. That does not mean that you have to remain the same forever. In fact this is the first step of transformation: if you love yourself you will be able to grow quicker, faster.

CONTEMPLATION BEFORE SLEEP

God is always with us; the problem is from our side, we are not with him. If God were not with us we could not exist even for a single moment. He is our life, he breathes in us, he beats in our hearts, he is our consciousness. He is always with us, but we are not always with him.

The moment we are also with him a radical change happens. Then you become aware of the meaning, of the significance of the song of life. Then you become aware of how much has been bestowed upon you, how much has been given to you. Then great gratefulness is felt, and that gratefulness is the essential core of religion, the very soul of religion. Everything else is ritual. To feel gratitude is to be religious.

d a y **31**

This is the law of existence: truth cannot be conquered but can be invited. One has to be just a host for the ultimate guest. And that's what I call meditation: it simply makes you empty of all rubbish, it empties you completely so you become spacious, receptive, sensitive, vulnerable, available. And all those qualities make you passionately inviting – an invitation for the unknown, an invitation for the unnameable, an invitation for that which will make your life a fulfilment, without which life is just an exercise in utter futility. But one cannot do anything more than that: just an invitation and waiting.

This is what I call prayer: invitation and waiting in deep trust that it is going to happen. And it happens, it has always happened! This is the ultimate law of existence.

MONTH 6

You are the sky

The only thing that is essential is awareness. And people are lost in the non-essential. They have become oblivious of the essential, they are ready to sell the essential for the non-essential. That's how everybody has sold his soul for the non-essential. That's how everybody has sold his soul and become soulless.

d
a
y
2

Man has to be a lamp unto himself. Drop the whole idea that you can get guidance from scriptures, that knowledge is possible by borrowing. That is one of the greatest hindrances in the spiritual search. Nothing is needed from the outside. God has provided you with everything that you will need on the journey. You just have to seek within yourself: the light is there and only your own inner light can help you to distinguish the right from the wrong, can help you not to go astray, can help you to be always moving towards existence. Those who depend on others are simply wasting their opportunity. My effort here is to guide you, not to give you directions, not to give you certain character styles, structures, patterns, but only to help you to be yourself.

CONTEMPLATION BEFORE SLEEP

Dreams can be realized, all dreams can be realized. The ultimate of the dream, of being blissful, is so close by that it is very strange how people go on missing it. It is just within reach, and everybody's reach. You have just to grope for it a little bit and it is there.

But people don't grope, or if they do, they grope in wrong directions, so life remains unfulfilled. And to live a life which is unfulfilled is agony, is hell; that's what hell is. It is not a geographical place somewhere; it is a state of an unfulfilled psychology. When there is fulfilment, there is paradise.

day **4**

We are all hung up in the head. That is our only problem. And there is only one solution: get down from the head into the heart and all problems disappear. They are created by the head. And suddenly everything is clear and so transparent that one is surprised how one was continuously inventing problems. Mysteries remain but problems disappear. Mysteries abound but problems evaporate. And mysteries are beautiful. They are not to be solved, they have to be lived.

CONTEMPLATION BEFORE SLEEP

We are making such a hard effort to remain miserable. People don't see it. When they do they will laugh at the whole ridiculousness of what they have been doing to themselves. They are really doing great work to create misery in every possible way. They don't miss a single opportunity; they jump upon anything that can make them miserable.

This approach has to be changed. And life gives both opportunities to you. It gives you the day, it gives you the night, it gives you the thorns and the roses – it gives you both opportunities. And it is always balanced, it is always fifty-fifty; it depends on you what you choose.

And the miracle is that if you choose the thorns, sooner or later you will find there are no flowers because your mind will become accustomed only to thorns. You will only be able to see thorns, you will miss the flowers; you will simply not take any note of them. And the same happens to the person who chooses flowers: he starts forgetting about thorns, he takes no note of them. His approach becomes so positive and so affirmative that his whole arithmetic is different.

day **6**

Reach for any door...you can try to reach through peace, and bliss will come and love will come and compassion will come and a tremendous understanding of other people; forgiveness will come, a great humility, humbleness, egolessness, truthfulness, sincerity, authenticity; they will all bloom. Just reach from any one direction. Try to reach from love or try to reach from compassion. It does not matter; there are many doors to the temple of God. But at every door you will need the same key to unlock it – and that is meditation, that is awareness.

A Jesus and Buddha and Krishna and Mohammed and Lao Tzu and Zarathustra all meet at the very centre. The doors were so different. But as they enter inside they suddenly know that all doors are right. And the miracle of miracles is that they were all using the same key. The doors were different, the shape of the locks were different, their directions were different, but they were using the same key.

Jesus says to his disciples again and again, "Beware!" Beware means "Be aware." Buddha says to his disciples continuously, day in, day out, year in, year out...for forty-two years he was teaching a single word, 'right-mindfulness', another name for awareness. Krishnamurti simply calls it 'awareness'. Gurdjieff used to call it 'self-remembering'; that is a Sufi word. Kabir simply called it *smrati*, remembrance. There is no need to call it self-remembrance because when you are in a state of remembrance it is naturally of the self, of the centre. These are different words but they are used for the same key.

CONTEMPLATION BEFORE SLEEP

Man unaware of himself is a beggar. Man aware of himself is the greatest emperor possible, because the moment you become aware of yourself the whole kingdom of God is yours. It has already been given to you, it is just that you are asleep. It is there, but you are not looking at it. Your eyes are focussed on the outside.

Society really wants you to be dead, not alive. The whole effort is how to kill you and yet use you as an efficient mechanism. And society has succeeded: it has destroyed aliveness and replaced it with mechanical efficiency. Its whole interest is in protection, even at the cost of life. It is more interested in commodities than in human growth. Hence society goes on preaching to people to be peaceful, to be obedient, to be undisturbing, and it praises such peace as if it is something divine, something of ultimate value.

But one can become peaceful in this way only if one is stupid, if one can't see the cost one is paying for such a dead peace, which is not worth anything at all. He is losing his freedom, his intelligence, his joy, his love, his whole quality of being adventurous. His whole being is lost; he becomes a convenient cog in the wheel, a replaceable part. If A dies he can be replaced by B, if B dies he can be replaced by D or C, because they were not individuals, they were only functionaries. And all the religions have tried for this. There has been a conspiracy between the priest and the politician to destroy humanity.

A few people have rebelled against this, and it is good that a few people rebelled, but then they fell into another extreme. They dropped the whole idea of peace as useless, worthless, as a political strategy to dominate, and they were not ready to be dominated by anybody. They chose to be blissful, joyous. But a bliss without peace is feverish; it is excitement but tiring, and ultimately there is no fulfilment in it. But it is not the only alternative; it is the other extreme.

CONTEMPLATION BEFORE SLEEP

My effort here is to create a higher synthesis in which peace and bliss are two aspects of the same coin. Then a tremendously beautiful phenomenon happens: you have bliss but you are not hot, and you have peace but you are not cold. It is exactly in the middle, both warm and cool – cool compared to cold, warm compared to hot. But it is both together: it is peaceful bliss or blissful peace.

Then your being is whole, you are rooted in wholeness. To know it is to know existence. To know it is to know all.

We are not aware of how precious we are. We are not aware of the inexhaustible treasure that we are carrying within us. And because we are not aware of it we go on desiring small things, quarrelling about mundane things, fighting, competing for something trivial. The moment you become aware of your own inner beauty all this struggle on the outside disappears. Life becomes calm and cool. Life attains to a grace. One is no more interested in the non-essential.

d
a
y
10

Awareness is what the alchemists have been searching for: the elixir, the nectar, the magical formula that can help one to become an immortal.

In fact everybody is immortal, but we are living in a mortal body and we are so close to the body that the identity arises. There is no distance to see the body as separate. We are so immersed in the body, rooted in the body, that we start feeling we are the body – and then the problem arises: we start becoming afraid of death. Then all the fears, all the nightmares, come in its wake.

Awareness creates the distance between you and your body. It makes you watchful of both your own body and mind, because body and mind are not separate. Body-mind is one identity, the mind is the inside of the body. And when you become aware of body-mind you immediately know you are separate from both and the distance starts happening. Then you know you are immortal, you are not part of time, you are part of the eternal. You know there is no birth for you and no death either, that you have always been here and will always be here. You have been in many bodies because you desired too much.

Each desire brings you back into the body because without a body no desire can be fulfilled. If one is very much attached to food one will need a body; without a body you cannot enjoy food – souls are not known to eat food. So a person who is too greedy for food is bound to come back in a body.

CONTEMPLATION BEFORE SLEEP

Life is full of divine glory but we are unconscious. We are so deeply asleep that we go on missing the glory of it. It is the most perfect existence possible, the most beautiful, the most magnificent. It cannot be improved upon. But we are asleep; hence we cannot have any connection with it.

It is as if it is spring and the trees are flowering and the birds are singing and the wind is dancing through the trees...and the beautiful patterns they are creating around you.... You will not see the flowers, their colours. You will not see the dance of the trees and the wind. You will not even know that you are in a garden! You will have no connection with the spring. You will be enclosed within yourself. You may be having a nightmare and you may be suffering in your nightmare; you may be screaming, crying and weeping. It has no relationship with the reality surrounding you.

That's exactly the situation of man. Existence is always in spring, but one has to be awake to know it, to feel it, to live it. And once you have tasted of the joy that surrounds you, you are religious because great gratitude arises in you, and thankfulness and prayer.

day **12**

Put all your energies into one effort: how to be more aware. And if one puts one's total energies into awareness it is bound to happen – it is our birthright. But one should not be half-hearted. It can't happen half-heartedly, it happens only when you are a hundred percent in it, into it, when nothing is held back, when you have put all your cards on the table, the trump card included, when you are not hiding anything. When you put yourself in totally, it immediately happens.

And that happening is a great revolution. It transforms you from the lowest to the highest, from the gross to the subtle, from the visible to the invisible; it takes you from the mind to the no-mind.

And to live in the no-mind is to be wise. To function out of no-mind is to function out of wisdom. Then your life has beauty, a grace, a godliness. Then whatsoever you do is right. It can't be wrong; it is impossible to do wrong because you are so full of light and so full of insight, your vision is so clear and unclouded that it is impossible to do anything wrong. The right happens of its own accord. There is no need to cultivate any character. Just consciousness is enough; character follows like a shadow.

CONTEMPLATION BEFORE SLEEP

To know oneself is to know all. And that is the only thing I emphasize: no belief, no dogma, no creed, no church, no religion. By a simple process of inner observation you come to realize yourself. And the moment you know who you are, immediately you know the essential core of the whole existence, of life itself, because you are part of it.

d
a
y

13

*d
a
y*

14

Life can be either just a heap of flowers or it can be transformed into a garland. Yours is just a heap of flowers, it has no organic unity, it is only a crowd of many selves, of many 'I's, all struggling and fighting for supremacy. Man lives in a constant inner war, and every self tries to pull you in a different direction. You are always falling to pieces.

Life can be lived in a totally different way. Those flowers which are separate can be connected by a thread, by something that runs through all of them, by a sense of direction, by awareness, by being more conscious. Then life is no longer accidental, then it is no longer a crowd; you start having an integrated being. And the more crystallized and integrated you are, the more joy is possible. How much bliss you will be able to receive depends on your integrity. The fragmentary person remains miserable, the integrated person attains bliss.

Become the thread so that you can join all the flowers of your life in a kind of togetherness, so life becomes not just a noise but an orchestra. Then there is great beauty and great bliss.

CONTEMPLATION BEFORE SLEEP

A humble heart is one of the greatest virtues for one who is in search of truth. Only those who are humble can know truth. The egoists are prohibited; the ego itself becomes the barrier, it cuts you away from existence. Ego means you are thinking you are separate from the whole. And you are not! We are not islands, no man is an island. We are part of an infinite continent.

The ego gives us a false feeling of separation, and because of that false feeling of separation slowly slowly we become enclosed in ourselves, we become too self-conscious, self-centred, utterly closed to the world, closed to the sun, to the moon, to the wind, to the rain. We become encapsulated; that is a kind of living death. We start carrying our grave around ourselves. It is a very invisible grave but it is a grave all the same.

day
16

We are small because we cling to the ego, our smallness is caused by our clinging to the ego. The ego is a very small phenomenon, and we are such fools that we go on clinging to it, thinking it is something immensely valuable. It is the only barrier, it is the only cause preventing our life from gaining significance, grandeur, glory. It is a subtle wall surrounding you which does not allow you to have a communion with the whole.

Once the ego is dropped, you start feeling one with the trees and the moon and the sun and the stars and the people. Suddenly all barriers disappear, suddenly you are no more a dewdrop, your boundaries are gone. You have become unbounded. And that's the experience of God.

CONTEMPLATION BEFORE SLEEP

Life in its reality is unbounded, it is infinite. It is not confined to the body, not confined to the mind either. It is not confined at all; it is oceanic. Even oceans have certain limits, but life has no limit at all, it has no beginning and no end.

But we have become too identified with the body and the mind. We have completely forgotten that this is not our reality. The body is only a caravanserai. We have lived in many bodies. You are the traveller, the pilgrim, the life, the consciousness that goes on moving from one body to another, from one mind to another, from one form to another. The day we realize that we are formless is a great day. That is the day of revelation. After that we are never the same again. After that we are part of God, and God is part of us.

d
a
y
18

Man is like a dewdrop. Existence is like the ocean, and we are trying to keep ourselves separate from it. That is the root cause of our misery. Only one thing is needed: jump into the ocean so the dewdrop disappears. It does not really disappear, it only loses its small boundaries. It becomes oceanic, it becomes the ocean itself. But in a sense it disappears. You cannot find it any more. It loses its old identity, its old nameplate and its old address. It has become part of such vastness that there is no way to find it, it cannot stand out. That is the fear. That's why we go on keeping ourselves away from the ocean. That day is the greatest day in life, when you die into the ultimate. It is not death. It is resurrection. Time dies, eternity is born. Finitude dies but infinity is born. Smallness dies but greatness is born. It is worth trying!

CONTEMPLATION BEFORE SLEEP

Just as a river dissolves into the ocean, dissolve into the divine. Don't think yourself separate from existence. Meet, merge more and more.

We go on insisting that we are separate. That is the only irreligious act: to emphasize separation. To emphasize unity is religion. It has to become a conscious effort.

Seeing a sunset, dissolve into it. Don't just remain an observer; let the observer and the observed become one. Slowly slowly you will learn the knack of it. Then sitting by the side of a tree you can have a deep feeling of unity with the tree. These small experiments can lead you ultimately to feel oneness with the whole, and that experience is God.

d
a
y

20

To remember that, "I am God," means to remember, "I am the sky." All the experiences that happen in life are like small clouds; they come and go, they are not worth paying much attention to. Take no notice. Let that be your meditation. Remember always you are the sky, the infinite sky, no clouds can distort you. Slowly slowly the clouds will not come to you. They never come uninvited. You may not have invited pain, but you invite pleasure, and pain is the other side of the same phenomenon. Invite one and the other comes. They cannot be divorced, they are always together.

When you stop inviting them these guests start disappearing. Soon a moment comes when you remain unclouded, and that's what Buddha calls nirvana, and Jesus calls the kingdom of God.

CONTEMPLATION BEFORE SLEEP

Meditation is the real beginning of life. The first birth is not the beginning of life. The first birth is only the beginning of an opportunity to live. The first birth only makes you potentially alive, not actually alive. That potentiality has to be transformed into actuality, then only do you become really alive. And meditation is the art of transforming the potential into the actual, of transforming the seed into the flower. It is through meditation that one attains the second birth.

With the first birth the body is born, with the second, the soul. And only when we come to know that we are a soul is our life fulfilled; otherwise it is a sheer wastage. The seed remained a seed; it never sprouted, it never became a tree, it never flowered. Nobody rested under its shade, no birds ever came to visit it, no winds danced around it. There was no dialogue with the clouds, the sun, the moon, the stars. The seed cannot communicate with existence. It is closed, encapsulated within itself.

Meditation opens you up. Meditation is nothing but opening multi-dimensionally to all that is: to the beauty of existence, to the music of the winds, to the freedom of the clouds, to all the mysteries that surround you, to all that is without and within.

*d
a
y*

22

People live in a very gross way, with anger, with jealousy, with possessiveness, with ego. One should remove all these gross elements from one's being because they are destroying so much energy, wasting so much opportunity. All these energies should be transformed into songs, into joy, into love, into peace. Then life becomes poetry. Then it is a sheer joy to be.

Just to be is more than one can ask for, just to breathe is enough proof that God exists, because each single breath brings so much ecstasy with it. Life becomes such a harmony and melody, such a dance that one cannot believe it is possible. One can believe only when it happens.

CONTEMPLATION BEFORE SLEEP

The ego is the only problem, and then it creates a thousand and one problems. It creates greed, it creates anger, it creates lust, it creates jealousy, and so on and so forth. And people go on fighting with greed, with anger, with lust, but it is futile. Unless the root is cut new branches will be coming up. You can go on pruning the branches and leaves. That is not going to help. In fact, by your pruning, the tree will become thicker and thicker. The foliage will also become thicker. The tree will become stronger.

My insistence is: don't fight with the symptoms, go to the very root of the matter, and that is simply one – it is the ego.

If you can learn just to be without the ego, to be as if one is not, to be a nobody, a nothingness, then the ultimate is achieved. There is no goal higher than that. And it can easily be done because ego is a false phenomenon; hence it can be dropped. It is not a real thing. It is imaginary, it is a shadow. If you go on believing in it, it is. If you look deeply into it, it is not found at all.

Meditation simply means looking deeply inside for the ego, searching every nook and corner of your being for where it is. It is not found anywhere. The moment it is not found anywhere it is finished and you are born anew.

Not to be is the only way of really being. So I cannot agree with Shakespeare that to be or not to be is the question. It is not the question at all, because not to be is the only way to be! The moment you disappear as an ego you become vast; you start experiencing some oceanic, unbounded ecstasies.

But we are attached too much to the mind, which is a very tiny thing, a very small biocomputer. And we are attached to the body, identified too much with it. It is just a small hut. Live in it, keep it clean, keep it beautiful. Use your biocomputer, take care of it as one should take care of every mechanism – and it is a very subtle and delicate mechanism – but don't become identified with these things. It is just like a driver becoming identified with his car. Of course he is in the car, inside the car, but he is not the car.

That's actually the case with us: we have become identified with the mechanism in which we are living. And this identification creates the idea of ego: "I am the body, I am the mind. I am Christian, I am Hindu, I am white, I am black, I am this, I am that...." All these things are nothing but identifications.

Meditation means becoming unidentified, just remembering, "I am only consciousness, a watchfulness, an awareness, a witness." In that witnessing the ego dissolves; and the dissolution of the ego is the greatest revolution. You are suddenly transported from a small, ugly world into the vast and the beautiful, from time to eternity, from death to immortality.

CONTEMPLATION BEFORE SLEEP

It is one of the greatest mysteries of life that we are born with perfect bliss in our being and we remain beggars because we never look into our own selves. We take it for granted, as if we already know all that is within. That is a great idiotic idea, but it prevails all over the world. We are ready to go to the moon to seek and search for bliss, but we are not ready to go inside ourselves for the simple reason that we already think without ever going in, "What is there inside?"

We somehow go on carrying this notion, that we know ourselves. We don't know ourselves at all.

Socrates is right when he says: "Know thyself." In those two words the whole wisdom of all the sages is condensed, because in knowing thyself all is known and all is fulfilled and all is achieved.

day 26

Jean-Paul Sartre has a very famous statement: "The other is hell." That's the idea of almost everybody in the world, except for a few buddhas: "The other is hell." I cannot agree with him, although it is the experience of millions of people. It looks absolutely right, but it is not right, not at all, not even an iota of truth in it. It is always *you*. You can be hell, you can be heaven – it is always you, it is your decision.

Heaven is not somewhere else; you have to create it just as you create hell. It is a psychological state. And once you know that you are the creator there is great freedom. If the other is responsible you are not free; you are always in bondage because the other can always create misery for you or can create happiness for you. In both ways you are dependent, and nobody likes dependence.

CONTEMPLATION BEFORE SLEEP

Man lives unconsciously; he goes on doing many things because others are doing them. He goes on following and imitating. He is not exactly aware of why he is doing these things, he is not even aware of who he is. What else can you expect when a man is not aware of who he is, from where he is coming, to where he is going and why?

These are the basic questions which can be solved only through meditation. No philosophy can help you to solve them. They will supply many many answers but all the answers will be hypothetical and if you ponder over them you can always find many flaws, many faults. Meditation is existential, not philosophical. It helps you to become aware so much so that you encounter yourself.

Truth is a revelation, not a conclusion of thought – a revelation in meditation, not a conclusion through meditation.

The pure heart is a basic condition for bliss to happen, but by purity I don't mean something moral; by purity I mean innocence. A moralist is never innocent, he is very calculating. His morality is nothing but his calculation. He is bargaining with God, he is earning virtue so that he can achieve paradise and the joys and the pleasures of paradise. He is really cunning, his morality is rooted in his arithmetic. He is not innocent; no moralist is ever innocent.

It sometimes happens that an immoral person may be more innocent than the so-called moral. The immoral may be immoral only because he has not calculated about his life. He is simply living, with no idea of the consequences. He may be simple, but the moralist is never simple, he is very complex. The so-called saints are the most complex, cunning, calculating people. You will not find the innocence of a child in their being – and that's what purity is.

A child is neither aware of the good nor the bad, that is his innocence. To become transcendental to good and bad again is purity, purity of the heart. The transcendence of duality is purity. The moralist chooses; the pure heart lives spontaneously without choosing. He lives in a choiceless way: fully alert, aware, but absolutely choiceless; available to the situation, responsible, responding – but not out of calculation. And that is the basic space in which bliss starts pouring in.

CONTEMPLATION BEFORE SLEEP

Purity is when you live in a choiceless awareness: when you are neither concerned with the good nor the bad, when you don't divide at all, when you accept everything as divine, when divisions have been dropped, when you see only the one. Even in the devil you see God and even in darkness, light, and even in death, eternal life. When the ordinary ways of seeing things as dual are dropped, you become pure because then nothing can contaminate you. That is the ultimate state of consciousness.

We have to transcend all duality: moral–immoral, good–bad, life–death, summer–winter. All have to be transcended so that one can see the one. One can see the one in so many millions of forms; one is capable of recognizing the one wherever, in whatsoever form it appears.

It is possible. All that is needed is a little effort to become more awake, a little effort to be aware and choiceless; just sitting inside, watching the mind, not choosing anything. The traffic passes on, you sit by the roadside unconcerned, cool. Slowly slowly a purity starts descending on you. That purity is liberation.

**d
a
y**

30

Learn awareness. Become more and more alert about everything that you are doing and about everything that goes on in your mind and moves in your heart. Be aware of all these three layers: the body, the mind, the heart – actions, thoughts, feelings. Be aware on all these planes and slowly slowly that awareness starts settling and the fourth is born in you. When the fourth is born God has penetrated you. The fourth is your soul, your innermost core. And the revelation of it reveals to you that you are unborn and that you are not going to die, that you are part of eternity.

And the very feel of eternity is ecstatic. Your whole perspective changes. It is the same world but it is no longer the same because you are no longer the same. Jesus says again and again, "Unless you are like small children you will not enter into the kingdom of God." But that does not mean that children are in the kingdom of God, otherwise they would not lose it. Who can lose the world of God, the kingdom of God for mundane things? They are not in it, they are unaware of it; hence the emphasis: those who are like small children. Remember the word 'like'; he is not saying those who are small children, he is saying like small children. One thing is certain, they are not children; they are like small children.

That's the definition of a sage: he attains a second childhood. And that's what sannyas is – the birth of a second childhood, this time with awareness. The first time it was without awareness and you lost it, but with awareness it can't be lost.

CONTEMPLATION BEFORE SLEEP

The true mystic is not an ascetic, is not self-torturing. He loves life, he enjoys life, because life is nothing but God manifest. A true mystic is full of songs. Each of his words is a song. Rightly understood, each of his movements is a dance; rightly understood, each of his gestures is a celebration.

This happens only because of the ultimate state of consciousness. When you have touched the highest peak, when there is no more beyond – when everything is left behind, the body far far away, down in the valley, mind also somewhere on the way, and you are just pure consciousness, no object, just pure subjectivity – that is called samadhi. And then thousands of songs will start arising in your being, thousands of flowers will bloom. And unless that happens, no man is fulfilled, no man can ever be contented, no man should ever be contented before this happens.

One should carry a divine discontent within one's heart.... One should become an intense longing to achieve samadhi, to achieve superconsciousness. It can happen to everybody. It is everybody's birthright, we just have to claim it.

MONTH 7

The heart is the garden of Eden

A man who has reached the ultimate truth, how can he lie, for what? There is no reason for him to lie. A man who has known truth is no more interested in ordinary worldly pursuits; he has known something higher than money can give, power can give, prestige can give. His whole life goes through a miraculous change.

The secret key that opens the world of miracles is blissfulness. Be of great cheer, let your heart sing and let your body dance and let your life become more and more a celebration.

CONTEMPLATION BEFORE SLEEP

Man, as he has existed for centuries – the common man, the ordinary man, the mob, the crowd – is mechanical. It is only through consciousness that you can go beyond this mechanicalness. And that is the real birth, then you become twice born. Through your parents you are only given a biological birth, not a spiritual birth.

The spiritual birth is only possible through the master.... With a master a totally different journey begins. You are given a birth, a new birth, a new dimension: the spiritual dimension. And it is given very consciously, very deliberately.

The whole work of the master upon the disciple is to bring him to some consciousness of his self, of his being....

Very few people have attained to their spiritual selves – and those that do are the only real men. Everybody has the potential but people never work on it, so it remains just a potential and it is lost.

It can become actual. So make it a point that from now onwards your whole life will become a concentrated effort to become more and more conscious. And as glimpses of consciousness start arising in you, you will be surprised: bliss follows each moment of consciousness. As consciousness deepens, bliss deepens. Bliss is the consequence, the by-product of being conscious.

We come into the world absolutely pure and inno-cent, absolutely clear, clean, but then the world starts writing on our consciousness, it starts conditioning us. It pollutes everybody, it contaminates, poisons. By the time a child is mature enough to think on his own the world has already destroyed him. He is already crippled, paralysed; the world has already taught him to use crutches and he has forgotten to use his own insight. He cannot stand on his own legs; it has made him dependent.

This is the greatest conspiracy against humanity, to make every human being a cripple – not physically but spiritually. And the strategy that is used is to give you a mind so that your consciousness becomes covered with thoughts, desires, ambitions. Ego, ideologies, religion, politics, and a thousand and one things are there, layer upon layer. Your mirror-like consciousness disappears and then a man lives a life of indignity, a life which is absolutely graceless, a life of blindness, a life of utter dependency.

And the only thing to be done is to undo whatso-ever the society has done to you. So I don't teach purity, I don't teach morality – that is all nonsense. I only teach meditation so you can get rid of the mind. The mind belongs to society and meditation belongs to you. With meditation you are absolutely free, and suddenly you start discovering your intrinsic treasures. And then begins a great pilgrimage of joys, beauty, songs, celebrations. And it is an unending process. It gives you the vision of eternity. It gives you the certainty that you are immortal.

CONTEMPLATION BEFORE SLEEP

Society needs every child to go through school, college, university – almost one-third of life is wasted – to force the energy towards an unnatural centre, the head, and to create barriers so that the energy does not go through the heart.

The natural process is that the energy comes from being to the heart and from the heart to the head. This is the natural process, and if the energy comes through the heart then the heart remains the master and the head becomes the servant. The whole trick of so-called education is to avoid the heart completely and to create a direct track between the being and the head and to ignore the heart.

It has been done; the heart is left by the side and the energy starts moving from the being to the head. Then the head becomes the master. And the head as a servant is a beautiful servant but as a master it is very ugly. The moment you understand what society has done to you, you can immediately open your heart and the energy starts flowing through it, because that is the natural way, it is how it should be. If the society had not interfered it would have been that way.

The society is very much afraid of love, very much afraid of heart, because if a person lives in the head he is efficient, a good servant, obedient, a slave – and that's what society needs: slaves, efficient workers, good servants. Society does not need masters.

Once your heart is opened even if you are imprisoned you remain a master. Your mastery is so deep that nothing can take it away from you.

So you have to do this miracle: shift your energy from the head to the heart.

d
a
y
5

Nothing is wrong with you except that you have believed in all kinds of fools, except that you have not listened to your own heart, and you have listened to all kinds of people who know nothing. Drop all that borrowed knowledge. Forget all about these stupid stories of original sin and forget all about your being a sinner.

Everybody is part of God, an intrinsic part. Everybody is divine. Yes, a few divine people are fast asleep – that is their choice. And a few people are awake – that is their choice. Nothing is wrong even in being asleep, you just have to suffer a few nightmares. But there is nothing much to worry about because those nightmares are just imaginary. Sooner or later you will wake up. And if you are enjoying it, enjoy! It is nobody else's business to interfere.

I would love you to wake up, but if you decide not to wake up, you are not to be condemned and thrown into hell. You are suffering enough just by being asleep, there is no need to make you suffer more in hell.

So this is the only difference between buddhas and the ordinary people; otherwise they are all alike...alike in the sense they all have the same potential to become awakened, not alike in the sense of being similar – they are unique.

CONTEMPLATION BEFORE SLEEP

Man ordinarily gathers dust around his being and loses the brightness which is his birthright. Everybody is born bright and everybody becomes mediocre. By the time one dies, one is almost stupid. This is a strange phenomenon. And people call it evolution – it is involution.

Children are more bright, more alive, more clear about everything, without any confusion. As they start growing they start gathering confusion from everywhere. We wait until they come of age then we give them the right to vote, because by that time everybody loses brightness, everybody becomes dull, stupid. Then you are called adult. You are really adulterated, completely adulterated. But people say, "Now you have become adult, you have come of age." Certainly politicians are afraid to give voting rights to children because they will see through and through. Voting rights can be given to you only when you have lost all capacity to see, when you are utterly blind.

My effort here is to help you to drop your rust, your dust, to cleanse your mirror, so you can again see your original face.

day

7

The whole structure of society is against the heart; it trains the head, it disciplines the head, it educates the head.

It neglects and ignores the heart because the heart is a dangerous phenomenon. The head is a machine. Machines are never rebellious, they cannot be. They simply follow orders. Machines are good in that way – they are obedient, hence the state, the church, the parents, everybody is interested in the head. It is convenient for all.

The heart creates inconvenience for the status quo, for the established order, for the vested interest.

Head functions through logic. It can be convinced. It can be made Christian, Hindu, Mohammedan, it can be made communist, fascist, socialist. Anything can be done with the head. You just need a clever system of education, a cunning strategy. Exactly the same as we feed the computers, we feed the head. And whatsoever you feed the head it goes on repeating. It can't make anything new, it is never original.

The heart lives through love, and love cannot be conditioned. It is essentially rebellious. One never knows where love will lead you. It is unpredictable, it is spontaneous, it never repeats the old, it always responds to the present moment. The heart lives in the present, the head lives in the past; hence the head is always traditional, conventional, and the heart is always revolutionary, rebellious. But you can be victorious only through the heart, through love, not through logic.

And the miracle is that when you rebel against the crowd psychology and you become more and more independent, suddenly you start feeling that you are becoming one with the whole, with the universal.

CONTEMPLATION BEFORE SLEEP

The whole history of humanity begins with the garden of Eden: man has been expelled from the garden and since then man has been wandering in a desert. He somehow remembers the glory of that garden, those days, those timeless days, before he was expelled.

The biblical story is not just a story, it contains a great truth. Every man feels that something is missing, that he is not where he should be. He may not be very clear about what is missing, but this much is felt by everyone, a vague feeling that something is wrong, that "I am in the wrong place, in the wrong situation," that "I am not supposed to be like this. Something has gone wrong."

Man was expelled from the garden of God. The reason for his expulsion was that he tried to be knowledgeable, he ate the fruits of knowledge from the tree of knowledge.

The moment one starts being knowledgeable one loses contact with one's heart – and that is the real garden. We are carrying it within ourselves. We are not really expelled, we have simply forgotten it, we have ignored it. We have become hung up in the head, we have become too attached to knowledge. Instead of growing in being, flowering in being, we are simply collecting information, sheer futile information.

The heart is the garden of Eden, the paradise. And my whole effort here is to help you in some way to enter the garden again. Once you have reached the garden, once you have tasted it again, you will be transformed.

day 9

Man can have knowledge but not wisdom. Knowledge is easy, you just need a little mind-effort, a little exertion. You can go on feeding your memory system. It is a computer; you can accumulate whole libraries. But wisdom is not something that you can accumulate because it does not happen through the mind at all. It happens through the heart, it happens through love, not through logic.

When the heart is open with love, with trust, when the heart is surrendered to the whole, then a new kind of insight arises in you, a clarity, a tremendously deep understanding of what life is about, of who you are, of why this whole existence exists in the first place. All the secrets are revealed, but through love not through logic, through the heart not through the head. God has a direct connection with the heart, no connection with the head at all. So if one wants to approach God the way goes through the heart.

Once you have known wisdom through the heart then you can use your mind also as a good servant, then you can even use the knowledge accumulated by the mind in the service of wisdom – but not before you have known through the heart.

Move your energy to the heart, be more loving and you are in for a great surprise. As your love grows, as your love petals open and your heart becomes a lotus, something tremendously beautiful starts descending on you – that is wisdom. And wisdom brings freedom. Knowledge brings information, wisdom brings transformation.

CONTEMPLATION BEFORE SLEEP

Humanity now knows more than it has ever known before: knowledge goes on accumulating. In fact you know more than Jesus. If you meet Jesus you can teach him many things. He will not know a thousand and one things.

But that does not mean that he is not a knower. He knows, but in a totally different way. His experience has transformed his being. He is not as informed as you are but he is transformed, and that is the real thing. Information means nothing. A computer can have more information than you have but the computer can never become a Christ or a Buddha. Or do you think a computer can become enlightened some day? I think that is impossible.

A computer can know everything possible but it will remain a computer and it will repeat only that which is fed to it. It cannot be blissful either – what bliss can a machine have? It cannot be loving either – how can a machine be loving? It may say, "I love you, I love you very much: I am ready to die for you." It may say beautiful things, but they will be simply words.

A machine can be taught these things and the machine can do these things very efficiently. But millions of people are doing exactly that: functioning like machines, computers. They repeat clichés – Christian, Hindu, Mohammedan – beautiful words but all dead.

The moment you start seeing on your own, your life takes a quantum leap into a new dimension: the dimension of eternity, the dimension of godliness, the dimension of bliss, truth, freedom.

day **11**

Knowledge is a dead thing, knowing is alive and flowing. In fact some day in the future we will have to evolve a totally new language because all our old languages are out of date. They were evolved by different people, for different purposes, in different situations. There things have disappeared but the language remains.

Now we know both religiously and scientifically that in existence there is nothing static. Everything is always in movement.

So instead of saying knowledge I say knowing, instead of saying love I would prefer 'loving'. But we have become so accustomed to nouns that we even call a river a river. It is just rivering; it is never the same even for two consecutive moments. We call trees, trees; they are growing each moment: some old leaves falling, some new leaves forming. Except for change, nothing is permanent in existence.

Start looking at life and not only looking but living also. Then knowing goes on and on. It is a pilgrimage which never ends. And the beauty is the wonder remains, the mystery remains. We go on knowing yet there is so much to know. Inexhaustible is existence and one can always remain like a child, full of wonder and awe.

God is a mystery and is available only to those whose hearts are dancing with wonder, whose being is thrilled with awe.

CONTEMPLATION BEFORE SLEEP

True knowledge, wisdom, happens through awareness – not by accumulating information but by going through a transformation. Awareness is a radical transformation; you are born anew.

Ordinarily one exists in a very sleepy state. One is aware very minimally, just one per cent or not even that. It is enough for your day-to-day work, it is enough to earn your bread and to make a shelter and to have children and a family. It is enough for that, but more than that is not possible. Ninety-nine per cent is just darkness in you. And all that darkness can be changed; one can be full of light. And then one knows the intensity of living, the tremendous ecstasy of living.

From this moment think of awareness as a question of life and death. In fact it is a question of life and death. Without awareness you are simply dying every day; with awareness you start living for the first time and then life goes on growing bigger and bigger, vaster and vaster.

One day it is so abundant that not only are you alive, whosoever comes close to you, he becomes alive. You start imparting some magic to others too, you start overflowing with life, love, light. And that is the state of a Buddha, of a Christ, of a wise man, of a wise woman.

Mind is incapable of knowing the truth. It can gather all kinds of information about the truth, but to know about truth is not to know truth. To know about love is not to know love; to know love one needs to be a lover. No information can be of any help; one has to go into the experience itself. And the same is true about truth. You can know all the great philosophers of the world, you can accumulate great words, theories, hypotheses and you can come to certain arbitrary conclusions of your own. But remember, they are arbitrary because they are not rooted in your experience. So whatever you know will hinder your search.

That is the greatest danger in knowledge: it can give you a false notion that you know. And once that wrong idea enters in you that you know, then the inquiry stops. One has to know that one knows not. One has to put aside all information for and against, theistic, Christian, Hindu, Mohammedan, religious, philosophical. One has to put aside every kind of knowledge, knowledge as such; then the inquiry begins. Then one becomes a true seeker of truth because then one is open. Out of that state of not-knowing, one day the great blessing happens that one comes to experience truth, to live it; one becomes it.

That is the state called enlightenment, nirvana. In the West they have called it the state of Christ-consciousness, in the East we have called it the state of Buddha-consciousness, but it is the same.

CONTEMPLATION BEFORE SLEEP

One has to be as innocent as a child; then and only then do the doors open. The doors of the divine remain closed for the knowledgeable people; for pundits, scholars, priests, the doors are completely closed. They already know, they don't need anything more. They have repressed their ignorance by accumulating borrowed knowledge. They have lost the quality of wonder, which is the most essential thing to God.

The child has tremendous wonder. His heart is continuously feeling the mysterious, the miraculous. His eyes are full of awe – at small things: pebbles on the seashore, seashells...he goes on accumulating them as if he has found diamonds. And he is intrigued by such small things – a butterfly, just a flower, an ordinary flower, and he is enchanted, almost hypnotized.

These are the qualities which help you to open to God, to bliss, to truth, to the mystery of existence. My sannyasins have to be just like small children.

day **15**

The wiser a person becomes, the more aware he becomes of how little he knows; the more stupid a person is, the more certain he is about his knowledge. You can judge the stupidity by the certainty. The stupid are very fanatical because they have arrived at ultimate conclusions. And not only have they arrived for themselves, they have arrived for everybody! They want to impose their conclusions on everybody, on the whole world. They think they are being very compassionate with people.

Socrates in his last days said, "I only know one thing, that I know nothing." And that was the day he became the greatest wise man the West has yet known. That day he became part of the great company of the buddhas. That day he was no more a philosopher, that day he became awakened, enlightened.

The head is full of conclusions, the heart is always innocent and always ready to know. The heart is always a child and the head is always an old man. The head is never young, remember, and the heart is never old.

CONTEMPLATION BEFORE SLEEP

Knowledge borrowed from others is untrue, knowledge gathered from the outside is untrue.

It hides your ignorance but it does not make you wise. It covers up your wounds but it does not heal. In a way it is very dangerous because one tends to forget one's wounds, and the wounds go on growing inside; they can become cancerous. It is better to know them. It is better to open them to the winds, to the rains, to the sun. Hiding them is protecting them, and they are your enemies. It is better to let them be exposed – nature heals. Hence the first step of true knowledge is to know, "I know nothing"; that is exposing your ignorance. And from that moment a turning happens, a great change happens: one starts looking inwards.

True knowledge has to happen within you. It can't come through thoughts, it has to come through a thoughtless space within you. It cannot come through studying, it comes through meditation. It comes only when the mind becomes absolutely contentless, so utterly empty and pure, uncontaminated, unpolluted, that your own inner sources start flowing because all the hindrances have been removed.

The source from where the spring can flow is there, but there are many rocks in the way, and those rocks are thought to be knowledge. They are not knowledge but enemies of knowledge. Drop all that you have learned from the without so that the within can speak to you, and then you will know the flavour of true knowledge, knowing. True knowing liberates.

day
17

Our body is small, our mind is small, but our being is vast – as vast as the ocean; in fact, vaster than any ocean because even the greatest ocean has its limits, and our being has no limits, it is infinite.

It has three qualities. The first quality is truth. When you experience your being for the first time you taste something of truth. Before that you had known only theories about truth. It was like a man who has known much about food, but has no experience of eating anything at all.

Truth we have not known, we have only heard many theories about it. Those are all hypotheses. When you enter into your being beyond the body, beyond the mind, the first taste is of truth, and the second taste is of consciousness. Otherwise consciousness is only a word.

People are fast asleep, they don't know what consciousness is. They are not conscious at all, they are like robots, functioning like machines. And the ultimate, the third thing, is bliss, *anand* – that is the peak. As you go deeper into yourself first you encounter truth, then you encounter consciousness, and at the very core of it you encounter bliss.

CONTEMPLATION BEFORE SLEEP

The scientists say that a single memory system, a single human mind, can contain all the libraries of the world, that much capacity is there. But even if one contains all the libraries of the world one will not be a buddha. One will still remain the same fool, the same donkey loaded with all the scriptures. It won't transform one's being. If one wants to transform the being one has to go beyond the word, one has to go beyond all theories, ideologies, doctrines, scriptures.

Be finished with information; put a full stop to it, because it only makes a man a parrot. We call those parrots *pundits*. But it does not make one contented, blissful, loving, knowing. Put an end to all information. That means put an end to the mind.

And putting an end to the mind is the birth of meditation. And once meditation is born then miracles start happening, then life starts taking such quantum leaps...unbelievable. One starts becoming aware of so many mysteries which are all around, which are so abundantly here. But we are closed because of our knowledge. Our eyes are closed. We are blind because of knowledge.

One has to become innocent like a child; and the moment one is innocent – clean, completely clean like a mirror – then one reflects the truth. And to know the truth is to become it.

We are brought up by every society, civilization, religion, in such a way that we are given a false identity. We are all deceived and cheated. And the people who cheat us are very powerful; in fact their power depends on their cheating and they have been cheating for centuries. They have accumulated great power – the politicians, the priests – and they are afraid of allowing anybody to know the truth. Their whole business depends on people who are gullible, ready to be deceived, very willing to be deceived – in fact asking to be deceived, hankering to be deceived.

From childhood they create such situations that slowly slowly the child becomes aware that if he wants to survive in the world he has to compromise. It is not a conscious decision – you can't expect that much consciousness from a child; even old people are not so conscious – but a vague awareness starts growing in the child that, "If I am going to be true I will be in constant trouble." If he says anything true he is immediately punished.

By the time you are strong enough to be truthful you have lost all sense of truth. Your lies have gone so deep in you, they have become so unconscious, they have become so much part and parcel of your blood, bones and marrow, that it becomes next to impossible to get rid of them. What society has done to you has to be undone. You have to be reborn, actually reborn; you have to start learning things from ABC, only then will you be aware that the ego is a false entity imposed on you, that you are not a separate unit at all, that you are part of the organic whole.

CONTEMPLATION BEFORE SLEEP

Children learn from their elders, so whatsoever the others are doing, children start doing.

Now our children are seeing movies and TV and murder and suicide and robberies, and all kinds of things. They are learning – they see violence everywhere, rape, murder – and they start repeating the same pattern. Their children will learn from them, it becomes a routine phenomenon – because we find that everybody is searching outside, though the treasure is within.

Jesus says again and again, "The kingdom of God is within," but even his very close followers never understood him. Even when the last night came and Jesus was going to be caught, they were asking about the kingdom of God in heaven, and for his whole life the poor man was saying that the kingdom of God is within you!

This was the last conversation with the disciples and they asked, "Just tell us one thing, master: in the kingdom of God you will be sitting at the right hand of God, and out of us, your twelve chosen disciples, who will be sitting next to you?"

You see the stupidity, the politics, the question of hierarchy. And the poor man has been saying his whole life, "Blessed are those who are not hankering to be first, because they will be first."

But people go on listening to words, beautiful words; they appreciate them also but they don't understand. We have missed Buddha, we have missed Jesus, we have missed all the great masters – that's why there is this miserable humanity.

day

21

Everyone brings a truth in his being. The truth has not to be invented, it has only to be discovered, or rather, rediscovered. We are already in possession of it, but we have become completely oblivious of the fact. We have only fallen asleep and forgotten who we are. All that is needed is a remembering.

You have to become more alert, you have to become more conscious. Nothing is missing, it is only that you are dreaming – dreaming that you are a beggar, and you are not a beggar.

Once the dream is broken, once you wake up, suddenly you find what ridiculous dreams you have been in. The greatest treasure is yours. Eternal life is yours. The kingdom of God is yours. The ultimate is yours. And we have brought it with ourselves. We are it! So it is not a question of seeking and searching somewhere else, it is simply a question of putting your total energy into waking up.

CONTEMPLATION BEFORE SLEEP

The joy of being truthful is such that who would like to fall into the darkness of being untrue? The simplicity of being truthful is such that who would like to create unnecessary complexities, complications, by being untruthful?

One lie brings in its wake a thousand and one other lies, because you have to defend it – and it cannot be defended by truth, it can only be defended by other lies. And every other lie will need in its own turn more lies. A single lie, and your whole life starts becoming untruthful, unauthentic.

Truth brings many gifts, but one has to open the door of meditation. Nobody can give you the truth; truth is already given to you from God himself. It is not something that has to be found anywhere else; it is already the case. You just have to take a few steps inwards.

Sannyas simply means this: a decision to find one's truth, a commitment that, "From this moment my life will be devoted to finding my truth."

The truth is not very far. It needs only one step, hence it is better not to call it a step: it is a quantum leap, a jump from mind to no-mind.

day

23

The story about Daniel is very beautiful. Mind you, I call it a story, not history, because to me parables, stories, are far more significant than history. History records only facts, parables record truths.

Daniel was cast into a lion's den for refusing to deny his faith, but he emerged unharmed. It says only one thing, that love for truth is greater than life itself, that one can sacrifice one's life for truth, but not vice versa. It also says that although man has evolved so much, still the basic instincts remain the same. Still people of trust are bound to suffer like Daniel, because society lives on untruths and it cannot tolerate a man of truth.

Secondly, it says that the man of truth need not be afraid; he cannot be harmed by anything, not even by lions, because the man of truth knows something which is eternal in him, indestructible. Even death cannot take it away.

To live for lies is worthless, to die for truth is one of the greatest blessings in life.

CONTEMPLATION BEFORE SLEEP

Truth cannot be purchased. There is no way to get it from others, it is untransferable. One has to discover it oneself. No money can purchase it, no power can purchase it, but if one enters oneself one finds it. In fact it is already given, there is no need to purchase it.

The irony is that everybody has purchased it. Somebody has purchased it from the Christian marketplace, somebody from the Hindu marketplace, somebody from the Jewish marketplace, somebody from the Gita and somebody from the Bible and somebody from the Koran. But remember, whatsoever you have purchased from others is only something about truth – it is not truth. You have purchased only words – empty, contentless.

Truth is truth only when it is your own experience. Jesus cannot give it, Buddha cannot give it, I cannot give it to you, nobody can give it to you for the simple reason that you have already got it. All that is needed is an inner search, an inner penetration to the core of your being – and you will find it!

It is good that it is not a commodity. It is good that nobody can give it to you; otherwise it would have been worthless. People would inherit it from their parents, people would write it in their wills: "Half of my truth will go to my wife and half to my girlfriend and it has to be divided equally amongst my sons...." It would be quite something. It is not – and it is good that it is not – a thing.

It is utterly individual; you know it in your absolute aloneness, your innermost shrine, the real temple, where truth is always waiting for you.

True religion is not based on beliefs; it is only the untrue religion that is based on beliefs. True religion is rooted in experience. All kinds of belief are barriers in experiencing the truth. If you already believe you stop inquiring. Once the belief is there you start thinking that you already know.

Belief simply means you have repressed all your doubts – and inquiry can begin only if your doubts are alive, fresh, young. Doubts are not to be repressed. They have to be used as stepping stones. They are not bad, nothing is wrong in them, but one should not live in doubts forever. One should use the doubts to find out the truth. And when you yourself find it has a totally different significance, it has a totally different quality to it. It is not impotent belief, it is living truth, it is your truth – you can risk your life for it.

CONTEMPLATION BEFORE SLEEP

Truth is always there, we are surrounded by it, but we are so perturbed inside that we cannot reflect it. The full moon is there, the stars are there, but the lake is so disturbed, there are so many waves, that it cannot reflect the full moon. It cannot rejoice in the full moon, it cannot rejoice in the stars. It remains blind to the sky which is just there. All that is needed is that the lake should become a little silent.

My whole effort here is to help you to make a silent lake of your consciousness. And it is possible. If it can happen to me, it can happen to you. I don't claim any extraordinariness. It can happen to anybody – just a little effort is needed, nothing else...no special privilege of birth, just a little effort, a little intelligence which is provided to everybody. And the moment you attain an inner silence, a radical change happens. Then you can say, "I rejoice!"

d
a
y

27

The only thing to be remembered is that knowledge does not consist of accumulating information. It does not consist of learning from others; on the contrary it consists of a process of unlearning. One really becomes a knower when one becomes as innocent as a child again. When the mirror of consciousness is absolutely contentless, when the lake of consciousness has no waves, no ripples even, then the whole sky, the whole existence, is reflected in you in all its glory, in all its beauty, in all its grandeur.

And that experience is God. Be empty, be still. In fact, be not. Be just nothingness so that the whole can descend in you, so that the whole can be reflected by your consciousness. That experience is the only religious experience, the only mystical experience. It gives you a certainty about God, not a belief but absolute certainty. It gives you absolute clarity. God becomes your own experience. It is not that Jesus says so or Buddha says so or I say so, but that you know it. The experience penetrates into your very guts, it becomes part of your being. Only then is the goal achieved and is life fulfilled.

CONTEMPLATION BEFORE SLEEP

If one is ready to become a nobody then one becomes the greatest. Be nothing then you are all, be nobody then you attain to tremendous extraordinariness. Just be empty and you will come to know the greatest in you, the highest in you. But remember: don't be nothing in order to become the greatest, because then you cannot be nothing. To be nothing is not to be used as a means to becoming the greatest. The greatness is a by-product, not the goal, not the end.

It is like a fragrance. The flower is the end, the flowering of your consciousness is all, and then suddenly there is fragrance. If you search for fragrance you will miss the flower, and without the flower there is no fragrance. If you search for the flower the fragrance comes of its own accord.

If one is meek, humble, nobody, then the doors of the kingdom open, then you are a divine guest. Then suddenly you are raised to the highest pinnacle of life. But that is a by-product. To attain the kingdom of God is not a goal. Forget all about it. My whole teaching is just to be a nobody. Just go on throwing out all the rotten furniture from inside your being and become utterly spacious.

And that space is overflowing, overflowing with your being, because the being can grow, it has space to grow. The being can open its petals, it can become a thousand-petalled lotus. And then there is a great dance inside and great music and great poetry and great beauty and grace. Then the whole imprisoned splendour is released because there is no barrier to hinder it. You become expansive. Life becomes an explosion of light, of love, of bliss.

day

29

We are taught from our very childhood to make a name in the world, to become famous, well-known, successful, a prime minister or a president, a Nobel prize-winner – but somebody special, somebody. Every child is poisoned with the idea of being somebody, and the reality is that we are nobodies. And the reality is tremendously beautiful! Just to be a nobody brings such joy and such ecstasy that one cannot even imagine it. Fame brings nothing. It is a very stupid game, very childish and immature.

My definition of real achievement is that which cannot be taken away by death. Anything that can be taken away by death is not a real achievement but only a pseudo achievement, toys to play with.

Become a nobody from this moment and enjoy nobodyness and the freedom that it brings. Become anonymous and see the joy! There is no worry, no anxiety. Because there is no ego you don't feel hurt. Nothing can hurt you. Somebody can insult you and you can stand there watching and enjoying it because there is nobody inside you to feel hurt, there is nobody to be wounded. You can enjoy and laugh.

The day a man can enjoy and laugh while he is being insulted he has already attained something, he has become part of eternity. He has entered into the world of the immortals.

CONTEMPLATION BEFORE SLEEP

If you have eyes to see you will be surprised: even a beggar is not just a beggar, he is also a human being. He has experienced love, he has experienced anger, he has experienced a thousand and one things which even emperors may be jealous of. His life is worth reading, worth observation, worth understanding, because his life is also a possibility of your life.

Each person is living a possibility, transforming a single possibility into actuality. And all those possibilities are yours too. You can be an Adolf Hitler and you can be a Jesus Christ – both doors are open. One has entered through one door, the other has entered from another door; both doors are open for you. Hence I have been as interested in Gautam Buddha as I have been interested in Adolf Hitler. I have been interested in Jesus but I have been interested in Judas too, because each human being is my possibility.

One has to understand this, then the whole universe becomes a university. That's exactly the meaning of university; it comes from the same word 'universe'. Then all situations become learning situations and all challenges become growth challenges. So slowly slowly one creates oneself.

We are born only as opportunities, then everything depends on us, what we are going to become, what the end result of it all is going to be.

d
a
y

31

The first seven years of life are the most important time. If the person is going to live seventy years then those first seven years are going to be decisive for seventy years, because he will repeat the same pattern on different planes. He will pretend to love his wife, he will pretend to love his children, he will pretend to love his friends. And the pretences will go so deep that he will not even feel that this is a pretence; he will think this is what love is supposed to be. This is love.

That's why everybody in the whole world is loving and the world is turning into a madhouse. People should be blissful – if there is so much love in the world everybody should be flowering. Nobody seems to be flowering. Something very basic is missing.

My effort here is to help you become aware of all your pretences. Once you are aware they can be dropped. They can be dropped very easily – the whole thing is to become aware of them. They have gone deep, their roots have reached very deep into your bones, into your very marrow. So one has to be very alert, very aware, to find all the roots. Once you have found all the roots of your false, pseudo love, you can uproot them. You can uproot all the weeds and you will become again a child and then you will start life afresh from the very beginning of innocence, and then there will be spontaneity, naturalness.

MONTH 8

Living one thousand per cent

L ove is the most shining star in the inner sky of your being. The outer stars are nothing compared to it.

The outer is beautiful, but nothing compared to the inner. And in the inner world love is the most shining star, the sun! It is the very soul of your inner world, the very source – go in and find it. And when you have found it, share it, celebrate it.

day **2**

If you forget what it means to be light you will forget what it means to be delight-full, because they are two aspects of the same phenomenon. To be light is a basic requirement for delight to happen.

Delight happens only in light moods. Don't take life as a problem – it is not a problem at all. It is a mystery to be lived, not to be solved – enjoyed, danced, loved, sung, but not to be solved. It is not a riddle which is a challenge to solve. It is a challenge to explore, with wonder, with awe, just like a small child.

So learn to be cheerful; take things as fun. Everything has to be taken as fun; even death has to be taken as fun.

CONTEMPLATION BEFORE SLEEP

Nobody is imperfect; hence nobody needs to be perfect. All that is needed is to live your life totally. Perfection is already there. We come from the perfect; hence we can't be imperfect. We are born out of the ultimate, we are waves in the ocean of God. So whatsoever is the quality of God is the quality of the waves. If God is perfect, we are perfect. So the very idea of becoming perfect is absurd. There is no need to become perfect, everyone is already perfect.

But we are not living that perfection in its totality, we are living at the minimum. We are not using our potential, we are using only a minor part of it – scientists say not more than seven percent. Ninety-three percent potential is simply lost. And it was already there, available for us to use.

When you live a hundred per cent you are really using the great opportunity that God has given you. And only at a hundred per cent does the transformation happen, never before it.

So my effort here is to make you love life as intensely as possible, to live each moment as wholly as possible, and slowly slowly something starts unfolding in you, and you start discovering yourself. The more challenges you give yourself, the more you discover.

**d
a
y
4**

You have to live in the world but you have to think of the world only as a big drama. I am against renouncing the world. You have not to escape from the world, you have to live in it, but in a totally different way. Don't take it seriously, take it very lightheartedly, take it as a cosmic joke. It is a cosmic joke. In the East we call it God's play. If it is God's play then we are just actors in it, and nobody takes acting seriously.

You can be a king in a drama, but you don't take it seriously. As the curtain falls you forget all about your being a king; it does not go to your head.

If you are rich, don't let it go to your head, or if you are poor, don't take it seriously. We are all playing roles: play them as beautifully as possible but continuously remember that it is all a game. And when death comes the final curtain drops. Then all actors disappear. They all disappear into one universal energy.

If one can live in the world remembering this, one is totally free from all misery. Misery is a by-product of taking things seriously and bliss is a by-product of taking things lightly. Take life as fun; rejoice in it.

CONTEMPLATION BEFORE SLEEP

I am proposing a totally new approach towards religion. Religion has to be life-affirmative. It has to enhance your life, it has to make it more beautiful; it has to be creative, not escapist. It has not to dull your senses but to make them more sensitive.

To me there is no God other than life itself, and there is no temple other than existence itself. Then everything becomes a divine celebration. And when I say everything, I mean everything: life is celebration, death is celebration; meeting is celebration, departing is celebration; childhood is celebration, youth is celebration, old age is celebration – different kinds of celebration.

If you start celebrating everything you become a real worshipper. And you need not believe in anything; you need not go to church or temple. Wherever you are, whatsoever you are doing becomes your prayer, becomes your meditation, becomes your *sadhana*, your discipline.

Love is the most healing force in the world. Nothing goes deeper than love: it heals not only the body, not only the mind, but also the soul. If one can love, then all one's wounds disappear. Then one becomes whole – and to be whole is to be holy.

Unless one is whole one is not holy. The physical health is a superficial phenomenon; it can happen through medicine, it can happen through science. But the innermost core of one's being can be healed only through love. Those who know the secret of love know the greatest secret of life. Then there is no misery for them, no old age, no death. Of course the body will become old and the body will die, but love reveals to you the truth that you are not the body, you are pure consciousness; you have no birth, no death. And to live in that pure consciousness is to live in tune with existence. Bliss is a by-product of living in tune with existence.

CONTEMPLATION BEFORE SLEEP

I am not much interested in God, in heaven, but I am absolutely interested in love, because the person who knows what love is, is bound to know what God is, but not vice versa. One may go on believing in God – one will not come to know what love is. In fact the believers in God have created so much hatred on the earth...nobody else has done so much mischief. Christians, Mohammedans, Hindus – they are all participants in a great conspiracy.

They talk about God, about peace, about love and all that they do is make bloodshed and nothing else. And for centuries that has been going on. In fact no sinners have committed so much sin as your so-called saints. They may not have done it directly, but they have provoked people to do such things.

Now when man becomes a little more alert and aware this whole thing will seem so ridiculous, so primitive and so stupid. And this has been done in the name of religion.

Hence my emphasis is on love, because if love happens then everything else happens. There is no question about it. A loving person cannot avoid encountering God for long. Even if he wants to escape he cannot escape; he will find God, he is bound to find him. It is inevitable.

d
a
y

8

One who loves is loved by the whole existence. Existence only echoes us from all directions, from all dimensions. If we sing a beautiful song the song comes back to us a thousandfold more beautiful, it showers back on us. Whatsoever we give is given back. People are miserable for the simple reason that they are giving misery to others, they are giving pain to others.

Whatsoever we sow we reap. And of course if you sow a single seed, you will reap thousands of seeds. Existence is not miserly, it gives abundantly, but it can give only when you have given already – it multiplies that which you give, so everything basically depends on you. If you want bliss, shower bliss on everyone, on everything. If you want love, love. If you want anything, wanting is not going to help – do it, materialize it, and soon you will be surprised, whatsoever you have given always comes back to you, multiplied a thousandfold, not less than that.

Whatsoever you want, give and you will not remain empty. You will be fulfilled, immensely fulfilled; beyond your imagination, beyond your dreams you will be fulfilled.

CONTEMPLATION BEFORE SLEEP

You get only that which you have because that which you have becomes a magnetic force; it attracts something similar to it. It is as if a drunkard comes to a city: soon he will find other drunkards. If a gambler comes to the city, soon he will become acquainted with other gamblers. If a thief comes to a city he will find other thieves. If a seeker of truth comes to the city he will find other seekers. Whatsoever we create in us becomes a magnetic centre, it creates a certain field of energy. And in that field of energy things start happening.

So if one wants existence's blessings one should create whatever blissfulness one is capable of, one should do one's utmost, and then a thousandfold bliss will be yours. The more you have, the more will be coming. Once this secret is understood, one goes on becoming richer and richer inwardly, deeper and deeper is one's joy. And there is no end to ecstasy – one just has to begin in the right direction.

day
10

Existence loves all. Existence is not indifferent to us, but it appears indifferent for the simple reason that we are indifferent. Existence only reflects. It is a mirror: it echoes us. If we shout at it, it shouts at us. If we sing to it, the song is returned. Whatsoever we do is returned in a thousandfold way, because it is returned from all the dimensions, from all the planes of existence.

It appears indifferent because we are not loving. Once you start loving all that is – the river, the mountain, the stars, the people, the animals – once you start getting involved in life with deep love, once you become warmed up the whole existence becomes warm towards you. It always pays in the same coin.

It looks meaningless because we don't create meaning. It looks as if it is very dull and drab because we are dull and drab. To a Buddha it does not appear like that. Buddha has said, "The moment I became enlightened the whole existence became enlightened." And I can vouch for him. What he says is absolutely true. That's my experience too: whatsoever you are, existence is that for you.

Meditation will teach you two things: meditation as far as your inner world is concerned; and love as far as existence is concerned. Meditation has to be your centre – awareness, a silent watchfulness; and love has to be your circumference, a warmth for no reason at all – because it is so beautiful to be warm.

At the centre be meditative, at the circumference be loving, and you will see the whole existence change. It is the same existence; in fact you are changing, but immediately, as you change, the whole existence changes with you.

CONTEMPLATION BEFORE SLEEP

Religion should not be a separate activity, it should not be apart from life, it should become your very life. Whatsoever one is doing – cooking, washing clothes, gardening – it is all prayer, it is all meditation, it is all celebration.

When religion becomes something apart from life it creates escapism. When religion means life then it becomes creativity. Take life as lightly as possible. The more lightly you take it, the closer you will be to enlightenment. The more lightly you take it, the more you will become full of light.

d a y

12

Peace is divine, it is God's gift. And God is very fair: if you are going into meditation earnestly, sincerely, you will be rewarded. There is no question about it, it has always happened that way. But this thing has to be remembered: peace is God's gift. We cannot do anything about it directly but we can create the right situation in which it descends from above.

It is like flowers: you cannot do anything directly about the flowers but you can prepare the ground, you can sow the seeds, you can help the plant to grow, and wait. In the right season, at the right moment the flowers will come; your effort will be rewarded. But you cannot pull flowers out of a seed, nor can you pull flowers out of a tree; you have to allow them to happen. They come from some unknown source, some mysterious source, but they always come. One has to be patient enough. One has simply to do one's work and trust that whenever the time is ripe the flowers will come.

They have always come. They came to Jesus, to Buddha, to Mohammed; they are going to come to you too. God has no favourites, he is neither for somebody nor against somebody. God simply means the ultimate law of nature. Just fulfil your task and nature immediately responds.

CONTEMPLATION BEFORE SLEEP

One should start enjoying just sitting silently, for no reason at all, with no motive at all – just for the sheer joy of sitting silently, just breathing, being, listening to the birds or watching your breath. Slowly, slowly a new fragrance starts arising in your being. That fragrance is meditation, that poise, that calmness, that stillness. It comes from beyond as a gift. And whenever someone is ready it always happens, inevitably.

Nature is never unfair to anybody. Whosoever deserves and whatsoever he deserves, he gets. If people are miserable they deserve it, that's what they deserve. Nobody is at fault, nobody else; nobody else is responsible – they have earned it.

If somebody is blissful that simply means he deserves it. Nature always gives that for which you have become worthy, for which you are ready and prepared and receptive to.

day **14**

Patience is a fundamental quality of the seeker. Impatience is a barrier in the search. You can't be in a hurry as far as God is concerned because God lives in eternity, and hurry means you are counting minutes and seconds and hours. That won't do. If you want to know God, if you want to know truth you have to know the way of eternity. That's why patience is needed.

Forget all about time, don't be in a hurry, don't be impatient. Wait. Wait lovingly with great expectancy but no expectation, full of joy that the guest may be coming any moment. But don't feel frustrated if he has not come yet. Keep everything ready to receive him. Go on preparing. If he has not come that simply means you are not yet ready.

So there is nothing to feel frustrated about. Just look around, prepare and prepare and prepare. The moment your preparation is perfect your silence is perfect, your emptiness is perfect, he comes – immediately he comes!

CONTEMPLATION BEFORE SLEEP

It is easy to be peaceful in a monastery. What else can you do there except be peaceful? But that peace is dead. It is closer to impotence. Then if one is impotent one can be a celibate quite easily. In fact what else is he supposed to do?

The world is a great challenge if you can learn the art of being silent amongst all distractions. Only then is your silence true, authentic, alive. And only through a peace which is alive can God come to you. God is life. A dead peace is absolutely worthless.

So be in the world but don't be of the world. Live in the world, but don't let the world enter into you. Move, pass through the world, but remain unaffected. It is possible. It is the greatest miracle but it is possible. And when it becomes possible one knows for the first time what ecstasy is.

day **16**

Everybody would like to be a man of peace, but just by liking one cannot become a man of peace. People go on shouting for peace and the same people go on preparing for war. The same people go on talking about peace and the same people go on piling up atom bombs, hydrogen bombs; they are not different people.

It is a very strange phenomenon. Man lives in such contradiction for the simple reason that it is easy to desire good and beautiful things, but to materialize them is a totally different thing. To dream is one thing, to make the dream a reality is another.

Everybody can afford dreams, and when you are dreaming you can dream beautiful dreams, but dreams are dreams: when you wake up they have not changed your reality even by an iota – the reality remains the same. And man becomes split: he dreams good things about godliness, about peace, about love, and he prepares for war, for destruction, for violence.

A real man of peace will have to go through an inner transformation, only then the dream becomes a reality. Meditation is the alchemy of transforming your aggressive energies into peaceful energies. It transforms your violence into love. They are not different, it is the same energy.

We have energies but we are not grown-ups. Hence our energies go berserk. Meditation is the process of growing up.

CONTEMPLATION BEFORE SLEEP

Hitherto humanity has praised hardness very much, particularly in man. For centuries man has been a male chauvinist pig! He has praised all that is aggressive, cruel, violent, warlike, and he has condemned all that is feminine.

And it is because of this a great problem has arisen. The problem is: all that is beautiful is feminine, and if you condemn the feminine then the beautiful disappears from the world. And we have struggled hard to destroy the beautiful. The ugly has dominated the beautiful, the hard has been praised over the soft.

Lao Tzu says, "Don't be hard like a rock, but be soft like water." He calls his way of life the watercourse way. And he says, "Ultimately the soft wins over the hard, the rock will disappear one day. Let the water go on falling on it and the rock will be reduced to sand." Of course, right now you cannot see it happening, it will take time, but the rock cannot destroy the water. For that one needs a little deeper insight – a longer vision, a bigger perspective.

And we are very short-sighted. We only see so far. Because of this short-sightedness the rock seems to be worth choosing, not water. Those who have seen reality in its true perspective of eternity, say something totally different.

Let softness be the gift.

MONTH EIGHT

d
a
y

18

Gentleness is one of the most divine qualities because the first requirement for being gentle is to drop the ego – ego is never gentle. Ego is always aggressive, it cannot be gentle. It is never humble, it is impossible for it to be humble. Its whole project crumbles if it becomes humble. And gentle is the way to reach existence.

One should be more like water than like a rock. And remember always: in the long run the water becomes victorious over the rock.

242

CONTEMPLATION BEFORE SLEEP

If your life becomes compassionate, that is the proof, a concrete proof that you have gone through an inner transformation, all tensions have disappeared and there is now absolute calm, absolute silence, absolute peace. You have arrived home. Compassion becomes the symbol, the criterion, the manifestation of what has happened at the innermost core of your being. Meditation happens inside, compassion is its outer expression, its manifestation. Nobody can see anybody else's meditativeness, but everybody can see the compassion, the love, that surrounds such a person. He becomes love, he becomes compassion.

Go deeply into meditation so compassion can be achieved. That is the ultimate truth of life.

d
a
y

20

Learn to be more and more silent, learn to be more and more still. Enjoy silence and stillness. Those are the basic preparations for the ultimate guest. When you are in profound silence you are capable of becoming the host to godliness.

CONTEMPLATION BEFORE SLEEP

Your religion has to be not out of fear, but out of love. Don't be afraid of hell – there is no hell, there never has been. It is a fiction created by the priests to exploit humanity, and they have exploited humanity for centuries. And there is no heaven either. Yes, there is a certain kind of hell and heaven, but that is psychological, within you. It has nothing to do with any place, somewhere below the earth or above in the sky. It is not geographical.

Drop the idea of heaven and hell – religion has nothing to do with all that nonsense. Drop the idea of God as a person. To call God the father is simply to provoke your fear, because each child has been afraid of the father from the very beginning.

There is no God as a person and there is no super-father in heaven. God simply means the whole existence, it is another name for life.

Love life, be devoted to life, live life as totally as possible. Offer yourself to life totally without holding anything back and then great bliss arises, bliss that has a beginning but no end.

day

22

When you move inwards, the people who have gone in cannot leave any footprints for anybody. It is impossible, because everybody's inner territory is so different that Buddha's footprints won't help you, and if you follow Buddha's footprints literally, you will never find yourself.

Jesus' map won't help you; you cannot follow it literally. It can help you in a very indirect way; it can make you aware of certain things inside, but in a very vague sense. It can give you the confidence that, "Yes, there is a world inside, no doubt about it, because so many people cannot be lying. Buddha, Jesus, Zara-thustra, Lao Tzu, Mahavira, Krishna, Mohammed – such beautiful people cannot be lying. They cannot be in a conspiracy, for what? They never existed together – in different ages, in different countries – yet they all speak almost the same language...." But you cannot follow it exactly because Buddha's inner territory is different. Each individual is unique, so unique that you have to discover yourself all alone; hence great courage is needed.

This is the greatest adventure in life, and one who goes on this adventure is blessed.

CONTEMPLATION BEFORE SLEEP

Life is music, mind is noise. And because of the noisy mind we are unable to hear the music of life. Unless we stop the mind and its noise we will never come to know the beautiful music of life.

When the achieving mind ceases, bliss is. When the achieving mind functions, bliss is not. That's the whole secret of all the religions, of all mysticism. If one can understand this simple secret there is nothing more to understand in life. It is enough – this is a master key.

MONTH EIGHT

day **24**

Music comes very close to the experience of godliness because godliness is the ultimate music of existence. It is another name for the harmony that exists in the universe. What we call music is only a tiny drop of it. But even though it is a tiny drop it contains the whole secret of the ocean.

That's the attractiveness of music: it releases meditation in you, it releases the imprisoned splendour. For a moment all the walls of the prison disappear, you are transported into another world. For a moment you transcend time and space, you become infinite, unbounded. That is the beginning, the beginning of a journey that never ends.

Music was born in deep meditation. Music is an effort to create on the outside the same circumstance as happens in deep meditation within you. Hence a real meditator is the true musician. He may play, he may not play. He may compose, he may not compose. But he knows the secret, he has the golden key, and the true musician is bound to stumble sooner or later on the fact of meditation. He cannot avoid it for long, it is inevitable because the outer provokes the inner, it challenges the inner music that is fast asleep. And the same music is hidden in the whole existence; hence I call music one of the most divine phenomena in existence.

CONTEMPLATION BEFORE SLEEP

Meditation is music, the ultimate music: music without sound, music of silence. It is far richer, far deeper than any music that we can create through sound because sound is after all, a disturbance. We can make the disturbance lovable, but still it is a disturbance. Silence means no disturbance, nothing stirs, but there is great music, there is great harmony in that wordless, soundless state.

Meditation leads into that state of silence, and unless a man knows that silence he is not aware of what he is carrying in his heart. He remains unaware of his own kingdom, of his own richness, of his own treasures. He remains a beggar while he can be an emperor any moment – just by turning inwards.

Science is alchemical: once you have penetrated the barrier of sound, once you have passed the barrier of sound and reached into the very core of your being you have reached the very centre of existence. Those who have heard it, they have called it by many names. One of the names is God.

God is not a philosophy, God is more music. God is not a theology, God is more poetry. God is not a hypothesis, it is more a dance. Start seeking God in these directions and you will be moving rightly, you will arrive home.

Follow music in the outer world and in the inner world. There is no need to go to any other temple, music is enough. Learn to listen to the music of existence: the wind passing through the pine trees, or the sound of water, or the ocean in a tremendous dance. Listen carefully, attentively, listen mindlessly, listen without thinking, so that it can penetrate to the very core of your being. And you will be surprised that what the Bible cannot give you, what the Gita cannot give you music can give you.

CONTEMPLATION BEFORE SLEEP

Man without meditation is a man without any song in his heart, without any poetry in his being, without any celebration. His spring has not come yet, his flowers are still waiting, they have yet to materialize, he has not yet bloomed, his fragrance is not released. He is just like a seed: encapsulated within himself – unaware, completely unaware of what he can be, of what he is. And he goes on living an ordinary life with no joy, with no bliss, with no dance. He drags himself along, life is like a burden; he somehow manages to carry it. In fact death looks like a relief that sooner or later everything will be finished and one will be able to rest in the grave.

Life is a school. We are here to learn something, and the most important thing to learn is how to sing, how to dance, how to rejoice; and all that becomes possible through meditation. Meditation releases all those energies in you. And thousands of flowers start blooming in your being. Then paradise is no longer after death, then paradise is now and here. And when paradise is now and here, only then is it a truth.

The first step towards truth is cheerfulness, a deep inner dance. One has to drop all that prevents that dance, one has to drop all that prevents one's life becoming a celebration. And we are all carrying many conditionings which are against blissfulness.

In fact religion has become almost synonymous with seriousness. Religious people look so sad, as if it is a sin to laugh. They cannot sing, they cannot dance, they cannot enjoy anything. They are against life. That is not the way to find the truth.

Love life, love the small things of life, the very small things. Eating, walking, sleeping – just the ordinary activities of life have to be transformed into delight. They have to be done with such joy that they all become a dance. Then truth is not far away, then each moment it becomes closer and closer. In the very moment your bliss is total, truth descends in you. And truth liberates.

CONTEMPLATION BEFORE SLEEP

If one can become laughter, if one can become love, then there is no need of any other prayer: one has already entered into the divine.

I have never seen any sad person enter into God. The only way towards God is the way of dancing. So learn to dance, sing, celebrate, rejoice; and then you will find God everywhere. Then each experience is divine and the ordinary starts changing into the extraordinary, the mundane disappears into the sacred. The whole of life becomes so God-full that it is not a question of some God somewhere above, in the sky. Wherever you are, you are surrounded by God. You are always walking on holy ground. Then each stone has a sermon in it and each rock is a scripture. One just needs a heart, a dancing heart, to see, to feel, to be!

day **30**

I am in tremendous love with the world and life, and I teach my sannyasins to be great lovers of life. Dance with the wind, dance when it is raining, dance with the trees, and you will be surprised that religion is not in the scriptures, it is spread all over existence. You may have its glimpses from a rainbow, you may have its experience from the dance of a peacock or a cuckoo calling from afar, or somebody playing on a flute.

Religion is not something dead. Religion is very much alive, and you have to be alive to make contact with it. If you live in misery, you live in death. If you live in bliss you become more and more alive. When your bliss reaches a peak, to an orgasmic peak, then you contact existence. And that contact gives you the proof that life is not only matter but something more. And that something more is indefinable. You can call it X, Y, Z, enlightenment, tao, truth, godliness, but these are just words to indicate something which cannot be contained in any word.

CONTEMPLATION BEFORE SLEEP

My whole vision is that of a dancing, singing, loving, laughing humanity. I would like to fill the whole earth with laughter, with music, with poetry, with paintings, with creativity, with more sensitivity. And the more a person is sensitive, creative, the more he is religious; the more he is creative the more he is close to the creator, obviously.

So rejoice in life – remember, that is my message to you!

MONTH 9

Dance your way to God

day

1

Wisdom is a song. It is not seriousness, it is playfulness; it is not sad, it is celebrating. And unless wisdom is a song it is not true. Then it is only knowledge, mere knowledge. It is only pretending to be wisdom. But real wisdom that can also become a song, that ultimately becomes a song, is born only out of meditation. There is no other way.

CONTEMPLATION BEFORE SLEEP

Life has to be rejoiced, life has to be lived in its totality. God has created this life and he does not seem to be an ascetic, otherwise why these flowers and rainbows and butterflies – for what?

God is not an ascetic – that much is absolutely certain. God is love, a creator, a poet, a singer, a dancer. He is not a perfectionist either: he loves growth, he loves inquiry, he loves people discovering themselves. He is tremendously interested in people growing on their own accord. He accepts that sometimes they will go astray; otherwise they cannot grow. And he accepts that they will commit mistakes; without committing mistakes nobody can ever learn.

God is not a saint – that much is certain. If there is any God he is going to be something like my sannyasin: utterly in love with existence and life; otherwise he would not have created. You have to learn a new kind of religiousness, a religiousness that can sing, dance, celebrate.

day **3**

Rejoicing in life is the way towards God. Dance your way to God, laugh your way to God, sing your way to God! And God must be tired of your serious saints by now. For centuries those stupid guys...either he must have committed suicide, seeing all those saints – I cannot even keep their pictures in my room – or he must have gone mad, or he must have escaped.

If you look at life, if this life is a creation of God, if this life is the expression of God, then God is a dancing God, full of flowers and fragrance, full of songs – very creative, sensitive – full of music.... If this life is any proof – and except for this life there is no other proof – then God cannot be a serious person.

CONTEMPLATION BEFORE SLEEP

Meditation makes you aware of great music – music without and music within. It is there, but we are not alert, we are not awake; hence we go on missing it. Otherwise the whole existence is nothing but music. That music is called 'God' by the mystics. God is not a person but the ultimate harmony of existence; it is an orchestra. Everything is in tune with everything else. The trees are in tune with the earth, the earth is in tune with the wind, the wind is in tune with the sky, the sky is in tune with the stars, and so on and so forth. There is no hierarchy. Even the smallest blade of grass is as significant as the biggest star. They both contribute to the orchestra of existence. They both enhance it, enrich it.

day
5

We have nothing to offer existence but we can sing, we can dance, we can play on some beautiful instrument. We can transform our whole life into a song, into a dance, into a festival – and that is the only true offering to existence. Plucking flowers from trees and offering them to existence is stupid, because those flowers are the trees', not yours; in fact they are already offered to existence by the tree. They were alive on the tree and you have killed them, you have destroyed their beauty. You are offering existence corpses.

You cannot offer words of Jesus to existence; they are his words, his songs. They are beautiful but they are borrowed. They have not arisen in your own heart, they don't have your heartbeat, they don't have your signature on them. You can offer beautiful songs of Krishna, Buddha, but all are borrowed.

My basic approach towards existence is that every person has to have his consciousness grow into a flowering tree. Each person has to come to some blossoming. And of course, man's flowers will not be like the flowers of trees; they will not be like roses or lotuses or marigolds. Man's flowers will be of love, they will be of freedom, they will be of joy, they will be of a higher quality. I call them songs.

When the singer loses himself in his song, in that moment he has offered the song to existence. When the dancer loses himself in the dance, the dancer has offered his dance. And when you start offering your joy, your love, your songs to existence, you will be surprised that the more you offer, the more is showered on you; a millionfold it comes back.

CONTEMPLATION BEFORE SLEEP

Everything is going on in such deep accord, but man remains unaware of it. That unawareness becomes his misery and he starts suffering from his own invented nightmares. Otherwise life is a celebration, it is a constant celebration, a continuum, a non-ending festival. We just have to become a little more silent to be able to hear it. And when we are absolutely silent, not only silent but when we are silence – then we disappear, then we are part of this whole cosmic harmony. That is the meeting of man with existence, of the part with the whole.

We disappear in one sense, we dissolve in one sense – as an ego, as a person – but we become the whole, so in another sense we are, for the first time. The dewdrop disappears but becomes the ocean. It is not a loser, it loses nothing. It loses only its small boundaries which were not worth keeping. In fact they were creating its whole trouble: the fear, the trembling, the constant fear that the sun will rise and it will disappear, it will die....

All our boundaries are in fact drawn by our death; we are defined by our death. The moment we lose our boundaries we lose our death too. Then we are eternal, then we are infinite.

Remember that meditation is succeeding if you become more and more alert to the great music that is always there – it just needs a sympathetic ear. Meditation creates that ear, that heart.

**d
a
y
7**

Our life is not worth calling life. Life starts only when you start moving in the dimension beyond death. That's what meditation is for: a strategy, a device, a ladder, to go beyond death. And just a glimpse of the beyond is enough. Then you know only the body is going to die, not you, and only the body is born, not you. You were here before your birth and you will be here after your death. You are part of eternity.

When one experiences this, life becomes blissful, and in that blissfulness one feels that existence has blessed one. Then naturally, spontaneously, gratitude arises. I call that gratitude prayer. All other prayers are pseudo. The real prayer arises only when you have experienced bliss and the blessing of it. Then naturally you have to be thankful, you have to bow down to existence. You feel what a gift has been given to you – and you had not asked for it, you don't even deserve it. Nobody deserves it, nobody is worthy of it, but existence gives out of its abundance.

CONTEMPLATION BEFORE SLEEP

Prayer is like a flower. Bliss is like the spring when flowers open up. And when the flowers open there is fragrance; the imprisoned fragrance is released. When prayer starts overflowing with no effort, naturally, spontaneously, when you are just thankful – for no particular reason at all, just to be is enough, just to exist for a single moment is enough....

To attain to that fragrance is to come to the peak of your life, to the crescendo. There is fulfilment and tremendous contentment. One has arrived home.

day 9

The ancient seers of the Upanishads have a beautiful prayer. It is one of the most beautiful prayers ever uttered. The prayer is *"Tamasoma jyotirgamaya –* Oh my lord, lead me from darkness to light; *Asatoma sad gamaya –* Oh my lord, lead me from untruth into truth; *Mrityorma amritam gamaya –* Oh my lord, lead me from death to deathlessness."

This is a beautiful prayer, the most beautiful prayer. But five thousand years have passed. I feel that now it needs a little improvement.

I would not say, "Lead me from darkness to light," because darkness does not exist. I would say, "Lead me from light to more light."

I would not say, "Lead me from untruth to truth," because untruth does not exist; I would say, "Lead me from truth to more truth."

I would not say, "Lead me from death to deathlessness," because death does not exist; I would say, "Lead me from deathlessness to more deathlessness, from life to more abundant life, from perfection to more perfection" – if that is possible, because ordinarily we think perfection means the end, but I don't think it is so. Perfection can become more perfect; perfection goes on becoming more and more perfect. At each stage it is perfect, but still that perfection is not a closedness, it is open. It can always become richer, it can always become more colourful, with new songs, with a new dance, with new celebrations. There is no end to evolution.

CONTEMPLATION BEFORE SLEEP

There are only two types of people in the world. There are the people who are always asking for more and never enjoying that which is available. When that which they are asking for becomes available they will still be asking for more. They are not going to enjoy either. They will be postponing their enjoyment for their whole life. Their life is nothing but a long, long postponement; it is always tomorrow. Today they have to work, today they have to earn, tomorrow they will relax and enjoy. But tomorrow never comes, it is always today. Hence they live without knowing what life is.

The second category is those who enjoy that which they have, not bothering about more. And the miracle is that every day they have more and more to enjoy. Their capacity to enjoy increases. They are constantly practising it, they enjoy each moment; they become more skilful in enjoying, they become connoisseurs of joy, they become very very sensitive about small nuances of pleasure. All their senses become alive, they become tremendously intelligent.

And out of this intelligence, awareness, sensitivity, the next moment will be born. Of course they will be able to enjoy the next moment more than they have enjoyed this moment. Their life will be a constant process of deepening; they will be moving into depth.

Man comes with all the potential of being a God and remains only an animal for the simple reason that he remains confined to raw energies. He never tries to change those raw energies into some refined form. They can be changed: anger can become compassion – it just has to pass through meditation; greed can become sharing, lust can become love, love can become prayer.

Yet we live at the lowest rung of the ladder, we live where we are born. We never think of ourselves as potential human beings, we take life for granted, as if we are already born entire, complete, perfect. That's not so. We are born with the capacity to be perfect, we are born with all the potential to reach the highest peak. But it is only a potential – it has to be made actual. And to make it actual you will need a certain methodology.

A certain science is needed, and that's the science of meditation. It is not a complicated science at all, very simple, but sometimes it happens that we go on missing the simplest thing in life. We miss the obvious because we are always looking far away. We are always attracted by the distant, by the far-away, and the closest always remains available.

Once you start going inwards, you will be surprised that it is such a simple phenomenon but it has tremendous beauty, the greatest joy possible, the greatest flowering possible. How had you missed it for so long? You will not be able to explain to yourself why and how you waited so long. And it can transform your whole being into gold.

CONTEMPLATION BEFORE SLEEP

Once you enter into the world of meditation, your vision, your perspective immediately changes. You start feeling that you are not here by accident, that you are fulfilling a certain need of existence.

Existence itself is behind you, but this can be discovered only in deep silence when your thoughts, your mind, your ego completely cease. In that clarity, when all the clouds have disappeared, the sun shines forth and in that light life is immediately transformed. It starts having meaning, significance, and with meaning and significance come joy, bliss.

day **13**

Just as every tree is rooted in the earth, every consciousness is rooted in God; God means the ultimate consciousness. And meditation is the bridge that takes you to the very source of your being. Once you have tasted the joy of being at the source, then everything else in life becomes meaningless. Then you can go on living the ordinary life but it is all acting, it is a beautiful drama. Play it as well as you can, but you know now that you are not part of it. It is just a role, it is not your existence.

Once the window opens you are transformed. And that's the whole purpose of sannyas: to open that window so that you can really know you are godly.

CONTEMPLATION BEFORE SLEEP

If you search within a man you will find him just a heap of no's: no, no, no. You can go on digging and you will find more and more no's, bigger and bigger no's. It is very rare to find a yes somewhere; and even if you find it, it will be paralysed, crippled. A poor yes will be killed, will be in a stampede! Even if it survives in some nook or cranny somewhere, it will be dying, not fully alive.

Life can become a total yes, but we have to change the whole pattern. All your no's can be melted and remoulded into yes. It is not so difficult as people think. Certainly it is not impossible. It has happened to many people – to Buddha, to Zarathustra, to Jesus, to Pythagoras, to Dionysius, to Lao Tzu. Around the globe it has happened to many people; it can happen to you. It should happen to everyone. In fact we are here for it to happen. And that's what I call the shift from a prose lifestyle to a poetry lifestyle, a shift from mathematics to music. And then life is a song, a tremendous ecstasy.

I don't teach a religion of sadness. I am against all those sado-masochistic religions. I teach a new kind of religiousness which is rooted in love, not in fear, which is rooted in the present, not in the future, which is rooted in love and not in logic.

A man can live life either as a no or as a yes. If you live your life as a no you become a warrior; you are constantly fighting. Then life is just a struggle, a war and you are fighting against everybody else. Of course it is a losing war, you are bound to lose. One cannot win against the whole; the whole idea is stupid. But it appeals to the ego. The ego always wants to say no. No is nourishment for the ego.

Yes is creative, yes is the way of the creator, the way of the lover. Yes means surrender. If no means war then yes means surrender: surrendering to the whole, trusting the whole as a friend – there is no need to fight – trusting life and existence.

Learn to say yes, learn to be yes, and a total yes. Don't hold back anything and don't make any conditions on the yes. And you will be surprised: life starts growing in leaps and bounds, life starts becoming such a splendour, such a beauty, such a grace that one cannot even imagine it.

Life can become an unending ecstasy. All that is needed on your part is to open your doors and windows. Say yes to the winds, to the sun, to the moon, to the rain, to the whole.

CONTEMPLATION BEFORE SLEEP

Ordinarily people live a closed life. They don't open their doors and windows. They live in fear, hiding, always afraid of the unknown. They don't allow the sun, the rain, the wind to enter their being. But if you put a rose plant in your room and you close all the windows and all the doors, and no wind, no rain, no sun reaches it, you cannot hope that the rose-bush will survive; it will die. That's how people are – almost dead. They are living a dead life, just dragging themselves along somehow.

To really live one has to be available to all that is. One has to be open and vulnerable, one has to drop all fears. There is only one thing to be afraid of, and that is fear. Except for that never be afraid of anything, because fear cripples, kills. The moment you start moving towards the unknown, in spite of all the fears, your life starts discovering many new things of which you were never aware, because as the adventure deepens, your thrill, your ecstasy deepens too.

As you start moving into the unknown there are so many challenges to be faced, encountered, that naturally you become more aware, more alert, more conscious. You have to be. It is walking on a razor's edge: how can you be sleepy, sloppy? You have to be cautious and alert, it is risky. And whenever there is risk, your intelligence becomes sharp. And when intelligence is sharp, ecstasy is great and you are thrilled at each movement.

Only in the climate of adventure, ecstasy, integrity, risk, danger, intelligence, awareness, does the inner being open, the bud become a flower.

day **17**

The moment you are not afraid of the unknown, the unknown immediately knocks on your door. If you are afraid then it does not disturb you. God never interferes in anybody's life because he loves his creation. So he leaves everybody total freedom, even to go against him – that is part of freedom. Even to close their doors to him – that is part of freedom. Even to deny him – that is part of freedom. But it is foolish to use freedom in that negative way. Use freedom in a positive way, use freedom to receive the unknown guest, use freedom to create trust and love and bliss so God can penetrate you.

And the meeting between your being and the being of the whole is the beginning of light, the beginning of eternal life, the beginning of immortality. And that is the search that everybody is on, knowingly, unknowingly.

Everybody wants to know something which is indestructible, which cannot be taken away. Everybody wants to come into light, everybody wants to have eyes to see, to have clarity of vision, but people go on doing things which really prevent their vision, hinder their insight, cripple their being.

CONTEMPLATION BEFORE SLEEP

If you choose the old you choose misery; if you choose the new you choose bliss. Let this be a key: always choose the new, the unknown, the dangerous, the insecure, because it is only through risking that one grows. And growth is bliss, maturity is bliss.

Never for a single moment cling to the old. Whatsoever is old go on dropping. The moment it is old be finished with it, put a full stop to it. Never look back, there is nothing worth looking back at. One cannot look back, one has to go ahead, always ahead. And be adventurous.

It is like climbing a virgin peak of a mountain – dangerous certainly, because nobody has travelled there before. You will have to create your way by going towards the peak. And of course there are many dangers, but danger is always beautiful because it is through danger that we become alert, aware, conscious.

Risk and danger and insecurity make you aware. And awareness is the greatest value because through awareness everything else comes in: love, joy, godliness, truth, liberation.

The most beautiful thing about danger is it gives you alertness, awareness; hence the people who go climbing an unknown peak, unmapped, are really seeking awareness. They are not aware of what they are searching for. The people who have reached the North and South Poles, taking all kinds of risks, the people who have gone to the moon, are not aware of what their search is really for. They are searching for awareness but not consciously.

A meditator goes consciously. There is no need to go to the Himalayan peaks or to the moon because there are higher peaks within you and greater distances within you and far more significant stars within you; the whole sky is there, the whole cosmos is there. But it is far more risky than going to the moon or going to Everest. The greatest, the most dangerous, the riskiest space is within; hence very few people dare to go there. Falling from those peaks which are inside you, you fall into a deeper abyss than you have ever known before.

But nobody ever falls from the peaks for the simple reason that as you move higher you become more alert, more conscious, you become aware of the razor's edge. You are like a tightrope walker who has to be aware, very aware. He cannot think of the past, he cannot think of the future. The moment is enough unto itself; he has to be here now. Hence there is no fall. I have never heard of anybody falling from the peak. But the danger is there, and because of danger very few people go into the inward world, the interiority of one's own being.

CONTEMPLATION BEFORE SLEEP

The outside world is not going to satisfy because it is a changing world, momentary, and our innermost longing is for the eternal. That cannot be fulfilled from the outside. So on the outside remain joyful with the momentary, don't ask that it should be eternal. Nothing can be eternal on the outside. Enjoy the momentary as momentary, knowing perfectly well that it is momentary.

The flower that has opened up in the morning is bound to die by the evening. It has come with the sunrise, it will go with the sunset. So rejoice! I am not against the flower – rejoice! But remember, don't cling, don't hope; otherwise you will be disillusioned. Rejoice in the momentary on the outside, and search for the eternal in the inside...and inside you will find *amrit*, nectar, the immortal, the eternal, the divine. And once you have found that there is nothing more to be found, then all is bliss, all is joy. Life is fulfilled. One has come home.

*d
a
y*

21

Man is a ladder – there are many possibilities in him; hence it is both a danger and a dignity, a glory and an agony. It is easier to fall; falling is always easier, no effort is needed for it. To rise needs effort. The higher you want to rise, the more effort is needed. If you want to reach the peaks of consciousness you will have to risk all.

One should not take one's being for granted because man has no being at all – just a spectrum of possibilities, the whole spectrum. That is the beauty of man, and his misery too. He is the only anxious animal in existence, the only animal who feels anguish. He is always at the crossroads; he has to choose every moment: to be or not to be, to be this or to be that. He is torn apart.

Sannyas is a decision, a commitment towards rising to the ultimate peaks.

CONTEMPLATION BEFORE SLEEP

Remain in the world but remain absolutely untouched, unidentified.

That's what sannyas is all about: living in the world and yet not being in the world, living in the world but not allowing the world to live in you, passing through the world fully aware that it is all momentary, so you need not get disturbed, you need not get distracted.

Then calamities and blessings, failure and success are all the same. And when you can see that darkness and light, life and death are all the same, a tremendous tranquillity, an equilibrium, a balance happens to you. That profound silence is truth.

day
23

To live within limitations is to live in gloom, in a state of indignity. It is a humiliation because our being needs the whole sky, only then can it dance, can it sing. Otherwise everything is crippled, paralysed; there is no space to fly, no space to move. And man lives in limitations: the limitation of the body, the limitation of the mind, the limitations of emotions, moods. These are all limitations upon limitations. And all these limitations have to be transcended....

Man should never become contented with any boundary. Whenever you come to a boundary try to go beyond it. When all boundaries are transcended, when you have reached infinity, you have come to existence, you have come home.

CONTEMPLATION BEFORE SLEEP

The lotus grows out of mud – the most beautiful flower grows out of dirty mud. It means that the dirty mud contains something beautiful. So don't reject the dirty mud, it contains lotuses. One cannot conceive that this beautiful flower, this delicate flower, with such fragrance, with such colour, has come out of ordinary mud.

Man is born as ordinary mud, but man contains a lotus – just in the seed. Man has not to be rejected, man has to be accepted and transformed. The world has not to be denied, because it contains something infinitely beautiful. It is not on the surface, it has to be brought to the surface.

Hence I am not against anything: not against the body, not against the world, not against the outside. I am not against anything, but I am for transforming everything. Whatsoever existence has given is something valuable; if we cannot understand its value it is our fault, our limited vision.

The second thing to be remembered about the lotus is: it lives in the water, but the water touches it not. It has such velvety petals that even if dewdrops gather on those petals they remain separate.

Live in the world but don't let the world enter you. Be in the world but don't be of the world. Remain aloof, remain cool, remain untouched. And then the world has much to teach you. The world is a device of existence; it is a situation in which to grow and mature.

Man ordinarily lives in darkness. We are born in darkness. In fact darkness is a basic need in the beginning. There is darkness in the mother's womb. It is needed because light will be a disturbance for the growing child. The child is soft, so tender; it needs velvety darkness around it. And the child sleeps for twenty-four hours a day in the mother's womb. In those nine months the child is growing so much that there needs to be no disturbance, otherwise energy will be diverted.

Everything in the beginning grows in darkness. You put the seed in the ground: you dig a little bit, then you put the seed in. If you just throw it on the ground it may not grow because there is too much light there. It needs the womb, the womb of the earth to grow in – there it is dark. Once the seed starts growing it starts rising above the earth. Then it starts reaching towards the sun, towards the moon, towards the stars.

The child is born. Physically he comes into light but spiritually he still remains in darkness. And that darkness can be dispelled only through meditation; hence meditation gives you a second birth. The first birth is physical, the second is spiritual. Physically you are in light, now you need another birth too – so that psychologically, spiritually also you are in full light.

Light is another name for existence. The moment you are born into that light you are enlightened. You are not two; you are not the seer and the light is not seen. You become one, you are the light.

CONTEMPLATION BEFORE SLEEP

Learn from the birds their song, learn from the trees their dance, learn from the rivers their music. And once you open up you will be surprised: the whole existence is such a poetic phenomenon!

One need not inquire into the meaning of it all; then it becomes a philosophical inquiry. The moment you ask, "What is the meaning of this?" you have lost track of poetry. The moment you start dancing with a tree without asking, "What is the meaning of this swaying tree in the wind?" you are being poetic. And the miracle, the miracle of miracles, is that the person who does not care about the meaning immediately finds it. Dance with the trees, sing with the birds, swim in the ocean, and you will find the meaning – without seeking it. Just become part of this beautiful existence.

Sing your song, because everybody has come with a song in the heart and unless you sing it you will remain unfulfilled. You have to do your thing – that's what I mean by singing your song. Whatsoever you feel like doing, do it! Don't be bothered about what others say, that is irrelevant. Insist that this is what you are going to do, irrespective of all the consequences. Don't compromise.

The poet is really a rebel, he never compromises. If he compromises he is not a poet, he is a businessman. And if you don't compromise, your love will grow in leaps and bounds. Sing your song and you will find love arriving from hidden sources within you. It will start overflowing from you, and reaching others.

d
a
y
27

When you are silent your potential speaks to you, whispers to you. And those whisperings are absolutely categorical – there are no ifs and buts. The heart knows nothing of ifs and buts, it simply says that this is your destiny: become a painter or a poet or a sculptor or a dancer or a musician. It simply says to you that this is how you will be fulfilled. It starts directing you.

The function of the master is to help you to be silent so that you can hear your own inner whisperings, and then your life starts moving through an inner discipline. So I don't give you any outer discipline. I help you to discover your insight; then you are free, then you move in freedom.

So sannyas is not a bondage, it is not a cult, it is not a creed. It is a declaration of freedom. It is a declaration of individuality. It is a declaration of love and creativity.

CONTEMPLATION BEFORE SLEEP

Don't think that a few things are mundane and a few other things are sacred. For the man who knows how to rejoice everything is sacred. There is no division between the world and God – it is all divine. Perhaps the world is manifest God and God is the unmanifest world. And when one rejoices, why make any difference between the manifest and the unmanifest? The flower is the manifest seed and the seed is the unmanifest flower – they are one. So is this world and that, this shore and that. There is no need to divide materialism and spiritualism – they are all together.

So rejoice in the smallest things: taking a shower or drinking tea. Don't make any differences. To the man who knows how to be blissful, drinking tea is as sacred as any prayer can be, his sleep is as sacred as any religious activity.

Cheerfulness brings a new vision, a new perspective. It transforms the whole world. Then chopping wood and carrying water from the well is as beautiful as the greatest activity.

So don't be sad and serious. Laughing, dancing, singing, live your life in a very simple and humble way, without any desire to improve, to attain something, to be ambitious, because life is so beautiful in its ordinariness that any improvement is going to destroy that beauty.

Song simply represents a state in which one is open and ready to pour one's heart into existence. The song is symbolic...that one is not miserable. The birds singing in the morning – just like them, one has to be constantly in the mood for singing, as if it is always morning, as if it is always the time for the sun to rise. Any moment the sun can rise and you have to welcome it, you have to be in a receptive mood. You have to be alert – the guest can come at any moment. The singing birds are just getting ready to welcome the sun. The flowers start opening, the trees start swaying. The whole earth becomes alive, aflame, ready to receive a new day.

The singing heart, the dancing heart, the loving heart, is ready to receive God. The miserable can go on praying, but out of misery the prayer goes wrong from the very beginning. It becomes heavy and falls back down on the earth. It has no wings; it cannot go to the ultimate, it cannot reach God.

When one is blissful, loving, when one is full of laughter, joy, when one is not serious about life but playful like a small child – innocent, wondering about each and everything, looking at everything with awe, when the heart is singing hallelujah – then God can come any moment. Learn how to be receptive, open, loving, singing, cheerful – and he is bound to come.

Jesus says, "Knock and the door shall be opened," and I say, "Don't bother! Just sing and he will knock on your door. He will say, 'Can I come in?'"

Make yourself so blissful that even God would like to come in. Tempt him rather than knock on his door!

CONTEMPLATION BEFORE SLEEP

The most fundamental thing is to know the nature of existence so that we can be in tune with it. Otherwise everybody is out of step, and being out of step is what misery is. To be in harmony with existence is bliss, to be in deep accord is bliss. To be in discord with existence is misery.

So the only thing which can bring a total transformation in your life is to become aware of the truth, the nature, the tao of existence. And the way does not go on the outside, the way goes through you; it is an inner journey. First you have to find your own centre. The moment you have found your own centre you have found the centre of existence because they are not separate. We differ only as circumferences, at the centre we are all meeting and merging. At the centre we are all one: the trees, the mountains, the people, the animals, the stars.

The moment you penetrate your own centre you come to know the tao of all that is. And once you have known the tao, nature, the dharma, you cannot go against it. That would be simply suicidal. But without knowing it of course one is bound to stumble, bound to go astray.

Meditation is a way to find your centre. The essential is meditation; if you can learn meditation you have learned all.

So many people seek and search for God without ever bothering about whether they are ready to meet him, whether they are ready so that he would want to meet them. They never think about that. My emphasis is: forget all about God, just prepare yourself. Whenever the time is ripe and you are ready, God is going to happen to you. You need not bother, you need not even think about God; your thinking is not going to help. Prepare, and to prepare means to rejoice, to blossom, to dance, to sing, to love, to meditate, so all the dimensions, all the petals of your being start opening.

MONTH 10

Bliss

Flow with the river, go with the river, abandon yourself totally to the river. It is already going to the ocean, it will take you to the ocean too; you need not even swim.

The ocean represents God, and unless we find the ocean we cannot be contented – because of the limitations, boundaries. All boundaries are bondages. The moment the river falls into the ocean it becomes infinite, it becomes eternal. And that is the goal of sannyas: to help you reach the infinite, the eternal, the vast, the unlimited, the indefinable, the ineffable.

day
_2_

Man builds his life on the sands of his dreams. That's why whatsoever one tries to do, everything fails, all houses collapse. They don't have their foundation in something eternal, they are founded in the momentary. And when one's house of sand falls we start making another house – of the same material, with the same material. We never seem to learn any lesson: if one dream fails we start dreaming another dream; if one desire is frustrated we immediately jump into another desire, another project – but we never see that desire as such is bound to fail.

To desire means to go against the whole. It is an impossible task, it cannot be done. Not to desire means to relax with the whole, to go with the whole, to have no desire of one's own; it means, "Whatsoever the whole wills is my will. I am not trying to achieve any individual goal."

We have to learn to be part of life, existence. We are waves in the ocean: we cannot have individual goals.

Meditation means coming to know that we don't exist as separate entities, that we are not islands; we are part of the infinite continent – call it God, call it truth, the ultimate, the absolute or whatever name you choose.

CONTEMPLATION BEFORE SLEEP

We are not separate from existence, but we all live with the idea that we are separate. The idea of separation is the ego. The idea, just the idea creates the whole hell, because then we become afraid for our own survival, become afraid for the future, we become afraid that one day we will have to die – and it is all concerned with the idea of the ego. We don't understand that we are one with the whole, that there has been no birth and no death, because we have always been here, part of the whole.

It is just like a wave which rises in the sea; it was there in the sea even before it rose – and when it has gone back to the sea to rest, it is still there. Birth and death are both false; the wave remains, sometimes latent, resting, sometimes manifest, but it is there, it is always there. It is part of the ocean.

We are also part of this existence, we are waves of this ocean, and once this is understood all anxiety disappears, there is nothing to worry about. This is our home – we are part of it. There is no way for us to be anywhere else or not to be – there is no way at all.

We can believe that we exist as separate entities, but that is only belief, not reality. And whenever belief goes against reality it creates suffering, because you live according to something which is not the case; you start going wrong. When you live according to the real there is no misery; bliss is the outcome.

If the leaf has consciousness it may start thinking it is separate, that it has nothing to do with the tree, that it will have its own way. And then immediately there will be trouble, there will be conflict.

It will become more and more alienated from its own sources of energy. The tree is its mother, and the tree is not only a tree, it is rooted in the earth; it represents the whole earth. It breathes the air, it represents the whole atmosphere. It is connected with the sun and with the farthest star. To fight with the tree is to fight with the universe. Just a poor, tiny leaf trying to fight with the universe – the whole idea is stupid. But that's what man goes on doing: he goes on pushing the river.

Sannyas means dropping the fight with the river, going with the river, allowing the river to take you, learning the art of let-go. Those two small, simple words 'let-go' define the very spirit of sannyas. Then one can say, "Thy kingdom come, thy will be done." Then one withdraws one's will, and the moment you withdraw your will your life becomes immensely rich. Suddenly the whole is with you – and we can be victorious only when the whole is with us.

CONTEMPLATION BEFORE SLEEP

Every child in the mother's womb is blissful. He has nothing there – he is not the president of the United States, he is not the richest man in the world, he possesses no palaces – he has nothing at all, but his bliss is infinite.

The psychologists say it is the bliss of the womb that haunts man all his life: how to regain it? We have tasted something in the mother's womb and we cannot forget it. We make every effort to forget it but somehow it lingers. It has been such a deep experience it is impossible to erase it.

But it can be attained again very easily. One just has to become like a small child and one has to think of the whole universe as the mother's womb. That's what actually a religion is supposed to do: to help you to think of the universe as the mother so there is no conflict between you and the universe, so that you can trust the universe, so that you know deeply that it cares about you, that you need not be worried and need not be continuously anxious, tense, that everything is taken care of. Then suddenly there is great bliss.

Meditation only helps you to fall back in the womb of the universe.

d a y 6

Truth is known only through a deep inner harmony. Ordinarily we are a chaos, very discordant, there is not one person in us but many. We are multipsychic; there are many minds inside, and they are all dragging us in different directions – many voices and you cannot figure out which is yours. One voice says, "Do this," another voice says, "Don't do this." One is constantly wavering. One is almost broken into thousands of pieces like a mirror thrown on the floor. That's the situation where man finds himself. But all those fragments can be gathered. They can be melted into the whole; they can be integrated, crystallized.

The moment that unity arises in you, great music is born, all noises change into an orchestra, and only then can you can see, hear, feel the truth of existence. It is always there but our minds are so noisy that we cannot feel it.

The moment this inner chaos is gone we can hear the still, small voice within. And then indubitably, unmistakably, one knows, "This is my voice, this is existence speaking in me." And there is never any doubt, you will not doubt it: it is indubitable. Only on that rock of indubitability, on that rock of certainty, can life become a temple – otherwise we are simply making sandcastles.

CONTEMPLATION BEFORE SLEEP

We do not become perfect, we are born perfect. And we do not invent bliss, we have only to discover it. Hence it is not such a difficult matter as people think; it is a very simple process of relaxing, resting, and slowly slowly, getting centred.

The day you stumble upon your centre, suddenly there is light; you have found the switch. It is just like groping in a dark room: you go on groping and then you find the switch. And that's actually the situation; we are unnecessarily crying and weeping.

Your suffering is simply foolish. It is like a man who has seen a rope as a snake, is running away and falls on a banana skin, breaks a few bones and may be in the hospital. You know that he was simply a fool – there was no snake at all!

This absurd, ridiculous life pattern has to be changed completely. Look within, and if you cannot find anything there, then look outside. But I say categorically that nobody who has looked within has ever missed it, so there is no reason for you to miss it. Nobody is an exception, it is an absolute law: one who goes within, finds it – finds the kingdom of God, the perfect bliss, the absolute truth. Life becomes a constant ecstasy.

One is bewildered at how much ecstasy is possible: "Can I contain more?" But one can contain infinite ecstasy. Unbelievable it is, because you think: "Now this is the limit, more is not possible," but the next day you discover that there is still more possible, and you go on discovering. It never comes to an end. There is a beginning to this journey but no end.

*d
a
y
8*

One can create hell, one can create heaven – it is our own decision, it is our own responsibility.

All the good things in life, in fact life itself, is a gift of God. So the problem isn't how to seek them but how to receive them. Take bliss – or receive bliss – for example.

It is not somewhere else far away in Tibet, in the Himalayas. It is not a question of travelling to it, the simple question is how to become more receptive. The gift goes on coming but finds our doors closed. The sun rises but we go on sitting in darkness because our eyes are closed. The gift is there – it is only a question of opening our eyes and all is light. But just by keeping the eyes closed we remain in darkness.

Don't remain closed to life and existence, become more vulnerable. That's all there is to religion – vulnerability, openness, trust. No need to be afraid of life; become available to it in all possible ways and you will be surprised that not even for a single moment was there any need to be miserable, one could have been blissful all along.

CONTEMPLATION BEFORE SLEEP

There are people who have become experts in finding reasons to be miserable. They cannot be happy unless they are miserable. They know only one happiness and that is that of misery. And when such people talk about their misery you can see in their eyes, in their face, in the way they are talking about it – everything shows – that they are enjoying it, they are bragging about it. They must be magnifying their misery, making it look as big as possible. Now how can these people ever be blissful?

Each moment always has both alternatives; you can choose to be miserable or to be blissful. Start looking at it in this way: in each situation, first try to find out what will make you miserable and what will make you happy about it.

d a y

10

When I was a small child, my father made a beautiful house. But the architect deceived him – he was a simple man – so the house collapsed in the first rains. We were just going to move into the house; just two or three days more and we would have been in the house, and the house collapsed. My father was far away; I sent a telegram to him, "Come immediately – the house has collapsed." He never came, he never answered. He came when he was expected to come and the first thing that he told me was, "You are a fool! That house is gone – why did you waste ten rupees in giving me such a long telegram? Those ten rupees could have been saved! And thank God that the house collapsed at the right time. If it had waited just four or five days more, then it would have killed the whole family!"

He invited the whole village for a feast. I loved that idea! The whole town laughed saying, "This is sheer nonsense: your house has collapsed, everyone is feeling miserable about it." And he called all the people of the town – it was a small town – for a big feast, to thank God for helping us. Just four days more and the whole family would have died!

This is what I call choosing, in every situation, the blissful part.

CONTEMPLATION BEFORE SLEEP

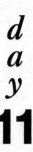

One of my sisters died. I loved that sister the most and I was miserable because of that sister's death – although I had ten other brothers and sisters. My father told me, "You are unnecessarily getting disturbed about it. Thank God that you have ten brothers and sisters still alive! He could have taken all of them. What can we do? Just as he has taken one he could have taken all. He has taken only one out of the eleven. That is nothing, that much we can afford. We can give one child to God; if he needs her let him have the child. But you have ten brothers and sisters – be happy that ten are still alive, rather than being unhappy for the one who has died." This has to be the approach of every religious person. Then your life naturally becomes a blessed phenomenon.

Each child knows how to be open, that's why all children are so beautiful and so blissful. Look into their eyes – so silent – and look at their joy – so over-flowing. Each child knows how to be blissful but forgets sooner or later. He forgets or we make him forget.

It can be relearned. Relearn the art, remember the art of opening up. And nothing is missing, nothing is imperfect – this is the most perfect world that can be....

Make yourself a lover of existence in all its manifestations. Then you will find sermons in stones. You will be surprised that there is really no need to look into the religious scriptures because the whole universe is the real scripture. Everywhere there is existence's signature on it and all those so-called religions are man-made.

d
a
y

12

Be cheerful – that is my definition of being religious. To be sad is to be a sinner, to be cheerful is to be a saint. If you can laugh whole-heartedly your life starts becoming holy. A whole-hearted laugh is something unique. Nothing can make your laugh more holy than a whole-hearted laugh. And when you laugh let all the cells of your body laugh with you. From the head to the toe let the laughter spread. Let it reach to the deepest, innermost recess of your being. And you will be surprised that one comes closer to existence more easily through laughter than through prayer.

CONTEMPLATION BEFORE SLEEP

Just today I was reading about an old man, ninety-five years old. He was asked what was the secret of his long life and his health. He said, "I feel a little embarrassed to say the truth. The truth is that I have been getting my life from the trees. I hug them and suddenly subtle flows of energies start entering my body. They have kept me alive and full of juice." And my own observation is that he is right. He may not be able to prove it scientifically but sooner or later it will be proved scientifically too: if you love a tree, the tree responds, if you love a rock, even the rock responds.

Experiment with love in as many ways as possible and you will become richer every day. You will find new sources and new ways to love, new objects to love. And then ultimately a moment comes when one simply sits with no objects of love, simply loving – not loving to somebody, just loving, just full of love, over-flowing with love. And that is the state of enlightenment. One is fulfilled, utterly contented, one has arrived. The feeling, the constant feeling that something is missing is, for the first time, no longer there.

And that is the great day in one's life, when you can feel nothing is missing, nothing at all. You search and you cannot find anything missing, all is fulfilled. That man has lived life truly. Others are simply wasting it, wasting a golden opportunity. We have to squeeze the juice of each and every moment to the fullest.

d
a
y

14

When you see a beautiful sunset and you feel joyous you naturally think that the joy is arising out of the beautiful sunset. That is not true. The beautiful sunset has simply triggered a process of meditation in you; it is so beautiful that your thinking has stopped. You are in a state of awe; it has possessed you. And the moment thinking stops you fall into deep meditation and you touch the source of joy within. But the logical mind infers that it was the beautiful sunset that caused the joy.

It has not caused the joy, it has simply triggered a process. Or even better is the word used by Carl Gustav Jung, 'synchronicity'. It has not caused it – because so many people may remain absolutely unaffected by it.

Synchronicity is not a cause, because millions may remain absolutely unaffected by the beauty of the sunset. Or there may be a few people who even become sad looking at it – it depends on them, their state of mind, their mood. It is not inevitable that one feels joyous.

Once this is understood then in each joyful moment you can immediately catch hold of a natural state of meditation. That's how meditation was discovered in the beginning. And it is always the same state; no thought, mind stops, and suddenly there is joy.

CONTEMPLATION BEFORE SLEEP

Tomorrow should be tomorrow, never today. You should not expect it to be the same. That very expectation is dangerous because in the first place it is never going to be so; hence you will feel frustrated. And if, by chance, by accident it happens to be just like today, then you will be bored, but frustration is not joy nor boredom joy.

Let the future be open. Don't put any expectations on it. Leave it unknown, unpredictable, and don't try in any way to make things permanent. The nature of life is change, and we have to flow with nature, with tao, with the ultimate law of existence.

Be in tune with it without any expectation on your part and you will be enriched tremendously. Each moment will bring you new joy, new life, new light, a new godliness. And a person whose love is always flowing and who is never confined by anything becomes vast, as vast as the sky itself. In that vastness one knows what existence is. That vastness is existence.

To live in the present is the only way to live at all. And when you live in the present with no past dragging you backwards and no future pulling you forwards, when your total energy is concentrated in the moment, life takes on a tremendous intensity; it becomes a passionate love affair. You become aflame with your own energy, you become full of light because at a certain intensity fire becomes life, intensity becomes light.

And that's the only way to be rich, to be prosperous. All others are poor. They may have all the money in the world but they are poor people.

There are two kinds of poor people in the world – the poor poor and the rich poor. Richness has nothing to do with possessions, it has something to do with how you live, the quality of your life, the music of your life, the poetry of your life. And all these things happen only through meditation. There has never been any other way, there is none and there never will be.

CONTEMPLATION BEFORE SLEEP

The only way to be rich is to become available to God's existence, to all his colours, to all his rainbows, to all the songs, to all the trees and flowers, because God is not to be found in churches – churches are manufactured by man. God is to be found in nature.

You will find him in the stars, you will find him in the earth. When it rains for the first time and the beautiful fragrance arises out of the earth you can find God there. You can find God in the eyes of a cow or in the giggling of a child. You can find God everywhere except the places that priests have invented. Churches, temples, mosques – these are empty, as empty as people are.

The moment one is ready to accept life as it comes with no conditions, suddenly God rushes towards one from every nook and cranny. To be full of God is the only possibility of having any meaning, any significance in life. And the person who has known God has known immortality. Then only the body will die; the essential core of his being is going to remain forever and forever.

d
a
y
18

People waste their whole lives thinking about God, arguing about God, and never listening to their heart. The heart has no desire for God. The heart only wants to dance, sing, enjoy, live, love, be loved. The heart wants to live like a flower full of perfume, like a bird flying into the open sky. The heart wants to become a torch, a light in the darkness of life. There is no desire for God. Unless you had been told by your parents and teachers and priests you would never have thought of God.

Hence I say bliss is God and there is no other God. All other gods are man's inventions, and it is better we drop them so that we can look in the right direction.

CONTEMPLATION BEFORE SLEEP

Love is the only bridge to victory. But a very strange bridge it is, because the first requirement of love is surrender. It is victory through surrender; hence it has a tremendous beauty. It is not aggressive, it is receptive; it wins not by conquering, it wins by being conquered.

Those who are trying to conquer God are fools, they cannot do it. The wise people have surrendered to God; they have invited him to conquer them.

God cannot be possessed by you but you can allow him to possess you. That's what love is: it allows one to be owned. It is non-possessive, love has no desire to possess. Its only longing is to be possessed, totally possessed, so nothing is left in oneself of one's own.

d a y
20

Love is the ultimate godly experience. Love proves that existence is not without meaning, that life has significance. Except for love there is no proof of life's significance. If one has not experienced love one will feel meaningless, accidental, just driftwood, at the mercy of the unknown, unconscious, natural forces. That's how materialists look at life: just a combination of matter, just a by-product of matter, an epiphenomenon. But then there is no significance, and without significance one can only drag oneself along, one cannot dance. Without significance only cowards can live. The courageous ones will commit suicide, they will commit hara-kiri.

Nobody really becomes convinced that life is meaningless because life is not meaningless; it has intrinsic value. But it has to be discovered. We are unconsciously, intuitively, instinctively aware of it. We have just a hunch that there is bound to be some meaning – but we are not clear about it. It has not come to light; we don't have any proof of it. Love gives us proof of it.

Love gives you a glimpse of meditation, and through meditation a window opens into the existence of God; hence I call love the most godly phenomenon on earth.

CONTEMPLATION BEFORE SLEEP

Love is the highest form of poetry – and by poetry I don't mean anything literal. To me poetry is far more than just composing poems. Poems can be composed even by someone who has no poetic life, who has no poetic grace. He can compose poems because to compose poems you only need a certain technique. He will be a technician, not a poet; and out of one hundred poets ninety-nine are technicians. And the same is true about every art: out of one hundred musicians there is only one who is a musician, ninety-nine are just technicians. And it is so about sculpture, painting, architecture, about every dimension of art.

The real poet has no necessity to compose poetry – he may, he may not. A real painter may paint, may not paint, but his life will be very colourful, his life will have a proportion, a symmetry, a balance. He himself will be his painting, he himself will be his poetry, he himself will be his sculpture.

That's what I mean when I say love is poetry: it gives you a new dimension; it makes you more aesthetic. It makes you aware of many things of which you were not aware before. It makes you aware of the stars and the flowers, and the green and the red and the gold of the trees. It makes you aware of people, their eyes, their faces, their lives. Each person is a tremendous phenomenon with infinite possibilities. Each person is an incredible story, each person is a living novel. Each person is a world unto himself.

d
a
y
22

Much is possible but it has to be made possible. All that is needed to make it possible is available but one has to work consciously on it. It is as if you have plenty of land and plenty of seeds and plenty of water and sun, but you never sow the seeds in the field. Flowers won't come and your land will remain a desert. Grass will grow, weeds will grow. That is one of the most important things to remember, that all that is useless grows by itself, and that which is significant has to be worked out. To achieve the significant is an uphill task. If you don't do anything weeds will grow; they will fill the whole ground. But then you cannot hope for roses and that was the promise. Everybody comes as a great promise but very few people fulfil the promises. They come empty-handed and they go empty-handed. It is a shame.

But my sannyasins have to go totally fulfilled. They have to actualize the promise that their life contains. They have to become that for which they are meant, they have to fulfil their destiny.

CONTEMPLATION BEFORE SLEEP

You cannot exist without the whole, and the whole also cannot exist without you. Just that you are is proof enough that existence needs you in some way, you are fulfilling a certain need.

Even the smallest blade of grass is as needed as the greatest star. There is no hierarchy in existence. Nobody is higher, nobody is lower, and nobody is more needed and nobody is less needed. All is needed because existence means the togetherness of all. We all contribute something to existence, and existence goes on giving to us everything we need.

The moment the ego is dropped nothing can go wrong. Nothing ever goes wrong: all is perfectly right as it is. That's exactly the meaning of God – that all is good as it is.

day

24

About love more is written than about anything else. In fact more is written about love than about God. So much poetry, so many songs, so many fictions, novels, stories – they are all concerned with the phenomenon of love. Why is humanity so obsessed with love? Films, television, radio, magazines, literature – are all concerned with love. It seems as if man is tremendously interested in love.

It is true, he is interested in love, but all these things are substitutes; he has not been able to experience it. He goes to a movie, sees somebody else in the act of love, becomes in a vicarious way a participant in it, forgets that he is just a spectator, becomes part of the story and enjoys it; he becomes identified with certain characters. Reading a novel he becomes part of the novel; reciting beautiful poetry he feels as if he is talking about his own experience. These are poor substitutes for the real experience.

If man really goes into love, all this nonsense will disappear from the earth. Always remember, only hungry people think about food, naked people think about clothes, people who don't have any roofs think about houses, naturally. We only think about things we don't have, we don't think about things we have.

It needs guts to be a lover because love demands one of the greatest things in life, surrender of the ego.

Then miracles start happening. Then love comes in, rushes in, fills you, and starts overflowing from you. And ultimately love itself becomes your experience of existence, your experience of truth.

CONTEMPLATION BEFORE SLEEP

The journey begins in love and ends in light or in enlightenment and the bridge is prayer. The whole pilgrimage from ignorance to wisdom is nothing but a pilgrimage of prayer.

Prayer means, "I am so small that nothing is possible through me unless the whole helps me." Prayer is a surrender of the ego to the whole – surrender not in despair but in deep understanding. How can the small wave go against the ocean? – the very effort is absurd. But that's what the whole of humanity is doing. We are all small waves in the vast ocean of consciousness. Call that ocean of consciousness God, truth, enlightenment, nirvana, tao, dharma – they all mean the same thing, that we are part of an infinite ocean. But we are all very small waves – we cannot have our own will and we cannot have our own destiny. The very desire to have our own will and to achieve something out of our own desires is the whole cause of misery.

Prayer means that in understanding the futility of human will, one surrenders to the divine will. One says, "Thy will be done, thy kingdom come."

It is possible only if there is great love for existence. Hence I say the journey begins in love and ends in enlightenment. And the middle of the journey consists only of prayer, of deep let-go.

The God of Moses says, "I am a very jealous God. Those who go against me will have to suffer eternally." The God of Moses is a very non-forgiving God. The idea is primitive, it is bound to be so. Moses was a pioneer, he was just breaking the ice.

Jesus took a quantum leap. Three thousand years after Moses he said God is love. He had to be crucified because he was sabotaging the whole Jewish religion. To make God love means to destroy the whole old idea, and the whole Judaic religion depended on it. Now two thousand years have passed since Jesus, and humanity needs a quantum leap again.

My experience is totally different: love is God – God is secondary, love is primary. In fact godliness is only one of the aspects of love, not vice versa. We can even drop the idea of God and nothing is lost. If one loves, that's enough, because love automatically brings a quality of godliness to your being, something of the beyond and the divine.

And it is time that we took a step further than Jesus. Two thousand years is enough! And if Jesus can take a step ahead of Moses, we should take a step ahead of Jesus. In fact by taking that step we are respecting Jesus because we are doing the same thing as he did.

Live according to your heart, live according to your love, let love be your light and you will never go wrong.

CONTEMPLATION BEFORE SLEEP

Religion is not theology, it is love. Theology is nothing but logic; hence it is called 'logy'. And logic has nothing to do with religion, in fact it is against religion.

Logic is a mind exercise, it is hair splitting, word-chopping. It can create beautiful, wordy edifices but they are just castles made in the sand; they are of no use. They can keep you occupied, they serve the same purpose as when you are sitting on a beach and you start playing with the sand and making sandcastles just because you have nothing else to do. You can enjoy the occupation but it is not beneficial at all, it is childish.

Theologians are never mature people. Jesus is not a theologian, neither is Buddha. No real master has ever been a theologian, but he is a lover, a tremendous lover, he loves the whole existence. Love is his prayer, love is his worship and through love existence can be communicated with, you can have a dialogue. All that is needed is a deep love affair, a mad, mad love affair....

The people who feel bored are the people who are living in the world of logic; logic is boring. But love is never boring. Love gives you constant surprises. Love keeps your wonder alive and love keeps your poetry, your dance, your celebration nourished; otherwise all that is beautiful in you starves, dies. Avoid logic and always choose love.

d
a
y
28

I don't teach any creed, I only help my people to be more conscious of everything that is within and without. That contains my whole teaching: be conscious, be aware and live out of your awareness. Let your awareness be decisive. Don't impose any discipline from the outside; let it spring from within, let it well up. And then it is always fresh, young, alive. And life becomes more and more intense, passionate. It becomes tremendously aflame with joy, with bliss, benediction.

CONTEMPLATION BEFORE SLEEP

Blessed are the blissful, because they have already entered into the kingdom of God. Not knowing that they are entering into God's heart, they have entered. In fact God can never be found directly. You cannot approach God directly, he has no address; he has no name either, no form. If you search for and seek God you will never find him.

It is because of this fact that humanity has slowly slowly, turned atheistic, because people have looked for God and they have not found him. They searched, they wasted their lives and finally they discovered it had been an exercise of utter futility.

But the whole responsibility falls on the shoulders of the priests, the popes, the *shankaracharyas*, the imams, the ayatollah, the so-called religious people, because they go on telling people to search for God, to seek God – and that is patent nonsense!

I say seek bliss and you will find God. Seek God and you will not find God, and you will become more miserable than you ever were before, because not finding something on which you have staked your whole life is bound to make you very frustrated. Forget all about God; just search for bliss. Find the causes of your misery and drop those causes, remove those causes from the very roots. And you will be surprised: as all the causes of misery are dropped bliss starts growing in you. And in blissful moments you will become aware of a new presence surrounding you – and not only you but the whole existence. That presence is God. God is not a person but a presence. God is not God but godliness.

day **30**

A man lives in defeat if he has not found bliss. His whole life is nothing but frustration and failure, writ large. And you can see it in people's faces: as they grow older they grow sadder; as they grow older they start becoming very angry, angry at life, because it has shattered all their dreams. And the fault is not life's, they themselves are responsible for it. They were trying to achieve things which are meaningless: money, power, prestige.

If you don't achieve them you are frustrated, if you achieve them you are more frustrated. In fact the non-achiever is in a better situation because he can still hope. One day he might achieve these things and then everything will be put right.

The achiever is really in absolute gloom because now there is no hope. He has staked everything on these stupid things; his whole life has gone into achieving all this junk and he is as unfulfilled as before.

Bliss is something of the inner, absolutely individual, personal; you can find it within yourself – nobody else is needed. And once it is found you are victorious. Then life has a great splendour. Then the whole sky of your being is full of stars.

And when one knows that one has not lived in vain then even death is beautiful. Then one does not die reluctantly, one dies absolutely blissfully. Then death is just a rest. One has blossomed, one has released one's fragrance; now the time has come to rest, to disappear in the whole. A sannyasin lives beautifully and dies beautifully. His life is a celebration and his death the ultimate in celebration.

CONTEMPLATION BEFORE SLEEP

d
a
y
31

The most significant thing about bliss is that it is intrinsically a paradox, and because of its paradoxical nature it has almost always been misunderstood. The paradox is: man needs to make much effort, and yet it does not happen because of the effort, it always happens as a gift of existence. But without effort man never becomes capable of receiving the gift. Even though the gift is always available, man remains closed.

So the whole human endeavour is not really the cause of attaining bliss; it cannot cause bliss; it can only remove the barriers. It is a negative process. It is as if you are living in a closed room, all the windows, all the doors are closed: the sun has risen but you are in darkness. The sun cannot rise because of your efforts. Whatsoever you do cannot make the sun rise, but you can open your doors or keep them closed – that much depends on your effort. If you open the doors the sun becomes available to you; otherwise it waits just on your doorsteps, without even knocking. You can live in darkness for eternity – and all that was needed was to remove the barrier between you and the sun....

A little bit of effort is needed and a little bit of trust is needed: a little bit of effort to remove the barriers, and a little bit of trust, patience, waiting – "God is gracious, so whenever my barrier is removed and I am ready, it is bound to happen, it is inevitable."

MONTH 11

Die to be reborn

Learn to be more and more aware: aware of your body, aware of your mind, aware of your heart; aware of your action, thought and feeling. These are the three dimensions to which awareness has to be brought. And when you are aware of all three you will become aware of the fourth – that is awareness itself. The fourth is the transcendence. The fourth leads you to godliness.

CONTEMPLATION BEFORE SLEEP

Man seems to be the only animal who does not learn from experience at all. That is my observation. Even donkeys learn.

In Arabic they have a proverb that even a donkey will not fall into the same ditch again...but can man do that miracle? He can fall into the same ditch thousands of times – never mind twice or thrice. Every time he passes by the side of the ditch he will fall in! He will say to himself, "Let me try once more – maybe things have changed, maybe it is not the same ditch, and certainly I am no longer the same person. So much has changed, and the last time it was evening and this time it is morning. So what is the problem? One more try...."

This is certainly the most important observation about man, that he never learns from his experience.

To be on the path of bliss all that is needed is to learn from your experience. Don't repeat the same stupid things – the same anger, the greed, the jealousy, the possessiveness. Don't repeat them. It is time to be aware, to be watchful, to be alert, and not to fall into the old traps again and again.

As you become capable of watchfulness, you become more and more capable of being free of all those traps. A moment comes when one is absolutely free from all traps and imprisonments – that is the moment of bliss. Bliss starts showering like flowers from the sky, and it goes on showering. One's life becomes a blessing to oneself and a blessing to others too.

day **3**

One has to work for bliss but still, ultimately, it is a gift of existence. This looks paradoxical; it is not logical, because logic will say either you have to work for it – then you are an achiever. Or it is a gift of existence – then you need not work because whenever existence feels like giving you the gift it will. But life does not go according to logic.

My attitude is that one needs effortless effort. There are reasons for thinking effort is needed, and perfectly valid reasons for concluding that the ultimate thing always happens through the grace of existence. It can be understood only in this way, that efforts are needed to prepare you to receive the gift.

Ordinarily you are not ready even to receive; your doors are closed, your heart is closed. Even if existence shouts you won't listen. Existence goes on knocking on your doors, but you never open them, you don't think there are any doors in fact. You go on living your ordinary, mechanical, unconscious life. Efforts are needed to make you conscious, but efforts can only make you conscious, they cannot give you bliss.

But whenever you are blissful that means something has descended from above. Those who have attained bliss have felt, "Our efforts have cleaned our heart, opened our doors, removed all the barriers. And then one day, suddenly, something poured from beyond, from some unknown source." And when you look back you can see that your efforts were very tiny. You cannot say this tremendous ecstasy is an outcome of your tiny efforts; still they were needed, they were essentially needed, they cannot be avoided.

CONTEMPLATION BEFORE SLEEP

Our roots are in our centre. If we are weeds the roots are in the centre, and if we want to become roses we have to grow the roots of the rose-bushes in the centre; the circumference will come to know the foliage and the flowers and the fragrance.

But you cannot move from the circumference to the centre; the movement is always from the centre towards the circumference. The circumference is just a shadow. And it is because for thousands of years religious people, moralists, and all kinds of reformists have been trying to change the circumference that they have created a mess of humanity; the centre remains the same.

The roots are of weeds and on the circumference we are hoping roses will come – they never come. Or, if we are very cunning, then we can purchase plastic roses and decorate the circumference. We can deceive others and finally we can deceive ourselves too. But plastic flowers are not real flowers. That's what the so-called moral character is: just plastic, synthetic. The real character has not to be cultivated, it is not to be practised; it comes as a natural consequence of meditation.

day
5

Die to be reborn! That's the meaning of the Christian symbol of the cross. But Christians have missed the meaning of the symbol, as all religions have missed the message of the founders. Buddhists have missed Buddha, Christians have missed Christ, Mohammedans have missed Mohammed. It is a very strange phenomenon that the followers go on calling themselves Christians but they are really killing the very spirit of Christ.

First the body dies. You start dropping the idea of a separate body; you can see the stupidity of it. Each moment existence goes on pouring new energy into you – how can you think yourself separate? If your breathing is cut off you will be dead! And it is not only breathing; every day you are taking in food and water, every day you are dropping out everything that has died; life goes on pouring in and dead things are thrown out of the body. That represents the first death, the first day.

Then the mind, which is a little subtler, thoughts – they also come from outside. Just as air and water and food come from the outside your mind goes on collecting thoughts from everywhere. The mind dies as a separate entity.

And then the most subtle thing happens on the third day – they are just symbolic these three days – feeling, emotion, the heart dies. And then there is resurrection.

When these three have disappeared, have become one with existence, suddenly you become aware of a being which is not yours, which is universal. That is resurrection.

CONTEMPLATION BEFORE SLEEP

Meditation is not doing at all, it is pure awareness. But a miracle happens, the greatest miracle in life. If you go on watching, tremendous and incredible things start happening. Your body becomes graceful, your body is no longer restless, tense; your body starts becoming light, unburdened; you can see great weights, mountainous weights, falling from your body. Your body starts becoming pure of all kinds of toxins and poisons. You will see your mind is no longer as active as before; its activity starts becoming less and less and gaps arise, gaps in which there are no thoughts. Those gaps are the most beautiful experiences because through those gaps you start seeing things as they are without any interference from the mind.

There are no more peaks and no more valleys, no more dark nights and no more moonlit nights; all those polarities disappear. You start becoming settled exactly in the middle. And all these miracles go on becoming deeper and deeper, and ultimately when your body is in total balance, your mind is absolutely silent and your heart is no longer full of desires, a quantum leap happens in you: suddenly you become aware of the fourth – of which you have never been aware before.

And that is you, the fourth. You can call it the soul, the self, God or whatsoever you want to call it, that is up to you; any name will do because it has no name of its own....

And in that moment all is light – your inner eye has opened. It is only through that inner eye and that light that one becomes aware of the truth of existence, and that truth liberates.

When all desires disappear you will not come back into the body but you will remain in the universal consciousness as part of the infinity. That's what we in the East call nirvana, the ultimate state of consciousness, when there is no need for any body, no need to be imprisoned again. We call it the ultimate freedom, because to be in a body is a bondage. Of course it is a very limited thing and you are unlimited; it is forcing the unlimited into such a limited, small world of the body. That's why there is constant tension, uneasiness, and one goes on feeling crippled, one goes on feeling crushed, crowded, imprisoned, chained.

One may not be exactly aware of it but vaguely everybody feels something is wrong. This is what is wrong: we are infinite and we are trying to exist through the very small world of the body.

Awareness frees you from the body. And the moment you know you are not the body, in that very moment all desires that can be fulfilled through the body also disappear. It is like bringing light into a dark room – darkness disappears. Awareness functions like light and all desires are nothing but darkness. And it is nectar.

CONTEMPLATION BEFORE SLEEP

There is a physical birth – everyone has passed through it – but it only gives you the body-mind complex. It only gives you an opportunity to be born spiritually. Unless the second birth happens one has not really lived. One was only an opportunity, just a seed, but the seed has never become a sprout, never become a tree. No spring happened for the seed, no flowering, no fragrance.

My whole effort is not to give you a formal kind of religion, not to give you a church or a dogma to cling to, but to give you a new being, a new humanity, a new consciousness.

One has to pass through two things. The first is a death, the death of the old, the death of the past, the death of the way you have lived up to now. And the second is a rebirth.

Start afresh, as if you were born today. It is not only a metaphor, it is so. You are born today. Let this sink deep into your heart so that you can become discontinuous with the past. Then the night is over and the sun has risen on the horizon.

day **9**

Man has three sources of energy in him. One is the body, the other is the mind, the third is the heart. Where all these three rivers meet, merge, become one, the fourth arises. You cannot call the fourth a body, nor the mind nor the heart; hence it is simply called *turiya*, the fourth. It has not been given any name. And the arising of the fourth is the beginning of the sacred, the transformation, the beginning of the real life, the authentic life, of life eternal, of divine life.

These three rivers exist in everybody but they rarely meet. In fact they go in different directions. The mind pulls to one side, the heart to another, the body has its own way. They never agree.

If you watch your inner workings you will be surprised: they never agree. The body says, "Stop. Don't eat any more, I am feeling too full," but the mind says, "The ice cream is so delicious – just a little bit more...." The heart says, "This is beautiful." The mind says, "You are just stupid, you are a fool, you are mad." Whenever the heart falls in love the mind says, "It is blindness," and whenever the heart moves in any direction, the mind always finds fault with it. They have different worlds.

The whole process of meditation is to help all these conflicting forces meet, merge, become harmonious with each other. Then you are full of energy because all that energy that was wasted in unnecessary conflict becomes available to you. And it is that energy which becomes wings and takes you to the beyond.

day **10**

They say, "You reap as you sow." If we are miserable that simply means that we have been sowing misery. Nobody else creates misery for you. Of course there is a gap between sowing and reaping, and because of that gap we think that somebody else is responsible. The gap deceives us.

Take the whole responsibility for your life. If it is ugly feel responsible for it. If it is nothing but anguish take responsibility for it. In the beginning it is hard to accept, "I am the cause of my own hell," but only in the beginning. Soon it starts opening doors of transformation, because if I am responsible for my hell, then I can create my heaven too. If I have created so much anguish for myself I can create so much ecstasy too. Responsibility brings freedom and responsibility brings creativity.

The moment you see that whatsoever you are is your own creation you are freed from all outer causes and circumstances. Now it is up to you: you can sing a beautiful song, you can dance a beautiful dance, you can live a life of celebration, your life can be a constant festival; nobody can disturb it. This is human dignity. God is a great respecter of individuals, and a person becomes an individual only when he takes the whole responsibility for himself upon himself.

d
a
y

11

Truth means experience. Truth is never a belief. Beliefs are always lies. They can make your life a little bit more convenient, that's all; they are like tranquillizers. Truth is awakening. And man needs awakening, not tranquillizers to fall into deep sleep. But for centuries man has remained attracted to alcohol, to other kinds of intoxicants, to psychedelic drugs; from the time of the Rig Veda up to now he has remained addicted. And all these intoxicants, psychedelic, alcoholic or whatsoever they are, are just efforts to avoid the truth. And to avoid the truth is to remain in misery.

Yes, we can make a life which is surrounded by misery comfortable, but it is stupid. We can have an absolutely blissful life but that is possible only if we drop the lies and inquire into truth. And the first requirement of the inquiry is not to carry any a priori ideas. Go in absolute ignorance, knowing nothing.

Whenever a person moves in a state of not knowing, he is bound to know truth. And truth brings bliss. My whole effort is to push you into inquiry, because it is inquiry, authentic inquiry, that brings a man to truth, to the realization of truth. And then bliss is yours, benediction is yours.

CONTEMPLATION BEFORE SLEEP

Man as an ego is a wound – he is sick, he is unhealthy. It continuously hurts; there is pain and anguish, there is misery, anxiety, darkness. One feels absolutely useless. But we don't allow this wound that hurts so much to be healed. We don't open it to the sun, to the rain, to the wind; we keep it hidden, we are afraid to expose it. We are afraid that somebody may know our wound.

And because we hide it, it remains unhealed. Because we keep it hidden behind layers and layers of hypocrisy it remains like a cancer, becoming bigger and bigger. And the bigger it is the more you have to hide it, and slowly slowly, the whole of your life becomes just a black hole.

That's what people are, just black holes. And they are responsible for the whole thing; this hell is their own creation. God is always ready to heal, the whole is always ready to heal. But we have to expose ourselves.

One has to stand naked, utterly naked before existence, with no secrets, no privacy, and immediately the healing happens. When it happens for the first time one cannot believe that the whole wound has evaporated so quickly. It is as if it never existed in the first place, as if it were just a dream, a nightmare. In fact that's what it is, a dream, a nightmare.

The healing is always done by existence but you have to allow it; you have to show it your wound, where it hurts. You don't deceive the physician, you have to tell him, whatsoever it is, however ugly it appears. Only then can he take the pus out, only then can he help the healing process.

Creating a character one becomes false, and split also. One becomes two persons because the very method of creating a character is that of repression – there is no other method. You have to repress your nature and you have to act according to certain principles decided by others. They tell you what is right and what is wrong, what is good and what is bad. They have already given you ten commandments and you have to follow them. Now what will you do with your nature?

You repress your nature, you neglect it, ignore it. But nature cannot be changed in this way; it goes on nagging you from within and forcing you to go against the character you have cultivated – hence all the hypocrisy. It is very rare to find a religious person who is not a hypocrite. And a person is really religious who is not a hypocrite.

Hypocrisy means you pretend to be something which you are not. You know it, it hurts; hence sadness. The whole world is full of sadness because the whole world has been directed to create character, morality.

I am not interested in character at all, in morality at all. I am not telling people to be immoral, I am telling people to be conscious, to create consciousness. And that's what meditation is meant for. It is a method to create consciousness. It makes you more alert, more aware, and as you become more aware your life starts changing.

Your doing and your being will have a deep harmony. And when doing and being are harmonious life is a joy, it is a dance.

CONTEMPLATION BEFORE SLEEP

Man has lived for centuries in lies – beautiful lies, but all lies. We go on believing in heaven and hell, we go on believing in God, in immortality, in the soul, but these are all beliefs – beliefs are lies. You don't know anything on your own, whether there is a soul within you or not. And it is not a question of argument; even if it is proved logically that you have a soul it will not make any difference to the quality of your life. Or if it is proved there is no soul, that will also not make any difference.

There are theists, there are atheists, and they are all living almost the same life. There are people who believe that God exists and there are people who believe that God does not exist, but if you look into their lives there is no difference.

And if you don't even know whether the soul exists within you or not, what else can you know? How can you know God and heaven and hell and all that nonsense? The closest thing to you is your soul, and you have not even explored that! And you are talking about some heaven somewhere above in the sky, and some hell deep down. You have no idea what you are talking about. In churches and temples and mosques people are continually arguing, discourses are being given about great things, and nobody bothers about the most simple thing – knowing who you are.

d
a
y

15

People live in comfortable lies. They don't want truth, they want consolations, cosy consolations; hence they remain clinging to superstitions, to traditions, to conventions, because all that is old has a certain prestige, a certain credit in the marketplace. All that is old, they say, is gold. It is not so.

The old looks gold only to fools, to the cowards.

Life is new every moment, it is never old. Existence is always now and here. It has nothing to do with the past and nothing to do with the future either. The moment you are also now and here there is a meeting – and that meeting becomes the truth. Of course it will shatter many illusions, it will shatter many ideologies, it will shatter all conceptions, all a priori beliefs, because truth cannot fit with you, truth cannot compromise with you and your ideas about it. You have to be ready to fit with truth itself.

That's what I call love for truth, a readiness to go with truth wherever it leads. And whatsoever needs to be dropped one is ready to drop, which is possible only if there is love for truth. Love can do everything, love can sacrifice everything. And truth requires total sacrifice, total commitment.

CONTEMPLATION BEFORE SLEEP

Modern man is living in such a hurry that he cannot sit, he cannot rest. He has become incapable of rest. And once you are incapable of rest you are incapable of all that is valuable. And the reality is that we need not be so worried about everything. Life is eternal. We have always been here and we always will be here; we are immortals. The body is going to change, the mind is going to change, but we are neither: neither the body, nor the mind.

It is only in deep meditation that one discovers the simple fact that we are not the body and the mind; we are awareness, consciousness. We are the witness of the whole game. Once you have known that witness you have tasted something of nectar. This is the nectar alchemists were in search of.

day **17**

Man ordinarily lives like a robot. He goes on doing things but he is not there. He eats, he walks, he talks, he listens – but he is not there. The mind is roaming all over the world: from the outside you may be sitting at the table taking your breakfast, but inside you may be on the moon...or any other stupid place. Not that one has to be on the moon...one can be almost anywhere. But one thing is almost certain, that you are not at the table. It is just automatic; you go on stuffing....

We have to de-automatize ourselves, we have to become a little slower in every act. So you have to be aware. When you are walking, don't walk at the old pace, at the old speed; slow down, so much so that you have to be alert, otherwise you will gather speed again. That is automatic....

Do everything very silently, very slowly, very peacefully, gracefully, so that each act becomes a deep meditation in awareness. If we can transform our acts into meditation, then meditation can be spread all over our lives, from morning to night.... The moment you wake up,become aware straight away: get out of bed, but be very alert.

You will forget many times in the beginning; remind yourself again and again. Slowly slowly, one gets the knack of it. Once you have got the knack of how to be aware in your day to day life, you have the secret key. And that is the most important thing. There is nothing more valuable than that secret key.

CONTEMPLATION BEFORE SLEEP

The whole past has been dominated by sad people. Sad people very much enjoy dominating others. They have no other joy; their only joy is crushing other people and their freedom, their only joy is in making more and more people joyless. They are very jealous and angry with people who are happy, who can sing and dance and rejoice.

These sad people have destroyed so much that it is almost inestimable. Nobody has done so much harm to humanity as these people – and these are the popes, the *shankaracharyas*, the ayatollahs, the imams. The whole priesthood of all the religions has been against humanity.

My effort here is to create a new man, and a new man can be created only with a new vision; only with a new vision of religiousness is the new man possible. I teach a religion of love, laughter, celebration. This is my own experience, that you are bridged with existence when you are blissful.

So I teach bliss and bliss and nothing else.

d
a
y

19

R emember two words: one is gravitation, the other is grace. Gravitation is the law of the earth, it pulls things down. Grace is the law of heaven, it pulls things up. Science discovered gravitation; religion discovered grace.

Ordinarily we are born and we live under the law of gravitation. Our whole life is a downward pull. We begin in birth and we end in death. We begin as fully alive and we end as a corpse. This is the downward flow.

Unless one starts moving inwards, the grace, the second law, cannot function. If we remain identified with the body then the law of the earth prevails; the body is part of the earth. When we start moving inwards – that's what meditation is all about – we become aware of something which is not part of the body. It is in the body, it is not the body. The body is only a temple, it is not the deity.

Once you have become aware of the inner deity that resides in the body, the second law immediately starts functioning; you are pulled upwards. Life becomes more and more abundant, more and more rich, more and more infinite, more and more perfect. It moves towards the sky, it starts becoming as vast as the sky, even the sky is not the limit. But the secret is in meditation.

day **20**

The body has a limitation, it is confined between life and death; and so is the mind. Mind is not separate from the body. It is its inner aspect; the inside of the body is the mind, the outside of the mind is body.

Languages give the false idea that these two are separate entities. It is not like body and mind. The truth is bodymind. It is one word, it is one reality. Just as every coin has two aspects and every wall has two sides, so is the case with bodymind. The body is limited, the mind is limited; hence the fear of death.

The body cannot be afraid because it is unconscious, but the mind can be afraid. The mind is constantly trembling. The fear is that sooner or later the full stop is going to come. And more than the full stop, the problem is that we have not achieved anything yet and life is going down the drain; every moment death is coming closer and life is slipping out of our hands. Hence the fear, the anxiety, the anguish.

One has to slowly disidentify oneself from the bodymind that surrounds us. It can be done. It has been done. And everybody is capable of doing it. It is not impossible – difficult certainly, but not impossible. And it is good that it is difficult because that gives us a challenge.

To rebel against all that is dead, unintelligent, is the greatest adventure, the greatest revolution. And it gives you a sharpness of the soul, of intelligence. In fact it creates an integrated individual in you and only in that integration do flowers of bliss blossom, bloom; you start growing. Otherwise people remain almost retarded.

The average psychological age of human beings is only twelve years. We are living in a retarded world. Even people who are eighty or ninety years old are only physically old; they have aged, but psychologically they are somewhere near about twelve.

Hence you can see that sometimes they forget their age and start behaving in a childish way. Give them a little more whisky than they are accustomed to and immediately you will see they have started behaving like a stupid child. Whisky cannot create stupidity, it has no chemical ingredients to create it. If it is already there it can expose it, that is true. It can only expose your reality, it cannot add anything to you, it cannot delete anything. It can simply help you to turn off your control, your repression.

Just insult somebody and within seconds he is no longer eighty, he is twelve, and he goes into a tantrum. He forgets all about his wisdom and experience.

Be courageous, courageous in a passionate, intense way, totally courageous, risking all, because unless you risk all you will not be able to know the hidden splendour of your life. When you risk all, your life for the first time opens to its ultimate maximum.

CONTEMPLATION BEFORE SLEEP

Unless we pour our whole energy into meditation it only remains a dream, it never becomes a reality. Meditation needs our totality. We cannot do it partially; you cannot do it only once in a while, for one hour a day or for fifteen minutes in the evening.

Transformation is possible only when the twenty-four hours of your day become a constant meditation, a continuum. So whatsoever you are doing – walking you are meditating, eating you are meditating, listening, talking you are meditating....

By meditation I simply mean an awareness. Whatsoever one is doing one is fully aware of each act – physical, mental, emotional – and then meditation becomes a twenty-four-hour-a-day phenomenon.

One day a miracle happens, and that miracle is that one can sleep with meditative awareness. The body sleeps but somewhere deep down a current of awareness continues; you are aware that you are asleep. A very paradoxical phenomenon, but it happens. On that day meditation has come to its completion, is known in its entirety. Unless that happens something is still missing. Only then can a person die meditatively. If you cannot sleep meditatively, how can you die meditatively? And the man who dies meditatively is never born again. He becomes part of the eternal cosmos, he lives in eternity, in existence. He is never thrown back again into bodily imprisonment.

day
23

It is not accidental that old people become very bitter. It is very difficult to live with old people, even if they are your own parents. It is very difficult for the simple reason that their whole life has gone down the drain; they are feeling bitter. They jump upon everything to throw their negativity. They cannot tolerate children being happy, dancing, singing, shouting out of joy – they cannot tolerate it.

In fact they are simply feeling bitter about the whole thing called life. And they go on finding excuses...it is very rare to find an old person not bitter. If there is an old person who is not bitter, that means he has lived really beautifully, he is really grown up. This old person has tremendous beauty which no young man can ever have. He has a certain ripeness, maturity, he is seasoned. He has seen so much and lived so much that he is tremendously grateful to existence.

But it is very hard to find that type of old man, because it means he is a Buddha, a Christ, a Krishna. Only an awakened person can be non-bitter in old age – because death is coming, life is gone, what is there for one to be happy about? One is simply angry.

Bitterness is a state of ignorance. You have to go beyond it, you have to learn the awareness which becomes a bridge to take you beyond. And that very going is revolution. The moment you have really gone beyond all complaints, all no's, there arises a tremendous yes – just yes, yes, yes – there is great fragrance. The same energy that was bitter becomes fragrance.

CONTEMPLATION BEFORE SLEEP

Evolution is an unconscious phenomenon. It is a natural phenomenon. The scientists say man was born as a fish in the ocean. Millions of years have passed between the stage of the fish and that of the human being. Man had to pass through all kinds of animal stages. The last stage before man was something like the ape, the monkey.

All this has happened unconsciously; no deliberate effort has been there. But since man became man that evolutionary process seems to have stopped. It seems that it has come to its culmination, because man has been man for thousands of years and no further growth has happened. It shows one thing, that nature has done all it could do; now we have to take it into our own hands. We have to move from evolution to revolution.

Evolution means unconscious, revolution means conscious. Evolution is growth but because it is unconscious it takes millions of years. Revolution is also growth but because it is conscious it is like a quantum leap, like a jump. It is not gradual, you don't go slowly step by step. It all depends on you, on how courageous you are. Even in a single step one can move from a human being to a God, to a buddha, to a christ. It all depends on your intensity, your commitment, involvement, your totality.

There is no possibility of man growing naturally any more; he will remain man unless he decides to grow consciously, deliberately, purposively. That's what sannyas is, a conscious decision to grow. And that is the beginning of revolution. Go beyond evolution and start a revolution in your life.

d
a
y
25

In a better human society we will tell every child, "You have the seeds of love, of bliss, of truth, but they are seeds. Your whole life has to be a tremendous effort to sow the seeds, to learn the art of growing, to be patient to wait for the seeds to sprout, then to take care of the plants and still to prayerfully wait for the right season when the flowering happens."

And that's what we are doing here. It is an experiment in inner farming, in inner gardening, in inner agriculture. But the first thing has to be the knowledge that up to now we have lived in vain and whatsoever you have done has been done from wrong ideas. And we have to wipe the slate clean, so the whole past is simply put aside.

Begin from scratch. It is as if you are born today and now you have to start living. Forget the past, don't go on carrying it. It has not given you anything. It has been tragic – no need to remain burdened with it. Become free of it so that you can experiment afresh.

CONTEMPLATION BEFORE SLEEP

Everybody is born blind and everybody has the capacity not to be blind. Everybody is born blind because at birth we are bound to be unconscious, unaware. It is only through life and its experiences, good and bad, painful and blissful, that one slowly slowly wakes up. It is only through a rich life – and by rich I mean a lived life. One who has been in the thick of life one day becomes capable of opening his eyes.

In that very moment one passes through a radical transformation. Then life is never the same again.

d
a
y
27

When you are with closed eyes all is dark. When you are with open eyes life is all colour, all light. God is the experience of existence with open eyes. Those who deny God are simply saying that they are blind. Not only are they blind, they are stubborn too. They are insisting that they are not blind but that there is no God.

If one keeps one's eyes closed, the sun may be there in the sky showering light but you live in darkness. Just a small curtain over your eyes is enough to prevent you from seeing the truth.

Life is the greatest teacher. It prepares everybody to take the ultimate jump from darkness into light.

CONTEMPLATION BEFORE SLEEP

The moment we are awake all miseries and all sufferings look so absurd, so foolish, so ridiculous that one wonders, "How did I suffer? And what was suffering? I suffered for so long – and all was false. There was no substance in it; it was just an idea, a dream."

Hence the mystics call our world an illusion, maya. Suffering is illusory, bliss is our true nature; remember it. And remember it again and again and again.

day
29

Man can exist in three ways: either like an animal or like a human being or like a God. Ordinarily people live like animals; there is not much difference. The only difference is that man is a worse animal than other animals, he can fall lower than any other animal. He is more cunning, more corrupt. He misuses his capacities. Rather than being creative he becomes destructive....

One is born as an animal. Very few become human beings. Humanity exists only in name, it has not yet arrived.

Only those people are human who have chosen, who have become decisive about their destiny, who have a sense of direction, who are creative, who are constantly discovering, exploring new ways of being and growth, who are not satisfied with the instinctive, who want to be intelligent in their lifestyles. They are human beings. And very few human beings rise to the ultimate, to be divine.

CONTEMPLATION BEFORE SLEEP

Man lives mechanically, just like a sleepwalker, a somnambulist; he goes on doing things but just like a robot. If you start watching your acts you will be surprised that you go on making the same mistakes every day. And you have decided many times not to do them again; but those decisions are meaningless. When the situation arises again, you react immediately in the old pattern. You don't know how to respond.

These two words are significant. Reaction means mechanical, unconscious, and response means non-mechanical, conscious. Response means according to the situation and reaction means acting according to the old pattern. Reaction means following ready-made answers, following a built-in program, being dictated and dominated by the past – that is reaction. And living in the moment, with no interference from the past, is response.

*d
a
y*

31

The only difference between the animal and the human is that the animal is absolutely unconscious, the human is a little bit conscious. And the only difference between the human and the divine is that the divine is absolutely conscious.

Man exists between the two: the absolute unconsciousness of the animals and the absolute consciousness of the buddhas, of the gods. One can either move downwards, fall back into darkness, or one can start climbing.

MONTH 12

*Man is not meant to creep
and crawl on the earth*

The body consists of darkness and the soul consists of light, and where this darkness and light meet, that is the territory of the mind. So mind has both a little bit of light and a little bit of darkness; hence mind always remains in tension, because it is being pulled in two opposite directions.

The body pulls it towards itself, the soul pulls towards itself. And both are almost equal magnetic forces so the mind remains hanging in between. Sometimes it chooses the body, sometimes it chooses the soul. But whatsoever it chooses there is always the feeling that it is wrong because the other has been left. There is a feeling that something is missing.

Mind continuously lives in choice. And every choice is going to be only half, and the other half will take revenge; hence mind is anxiety, anguish....

The mind cannot become part either of the body or of the soul. One has to get out of the mind to be free of the tension. Unless one transcends mind, goes beyond it, one cannot feel peace.

There is no such thing as peace of mind. People talk about peace of mind – that is nonsense. Mind means no peace, no-mind means peace. So the right expression will be 'peace of no-mind' – then you are centred in your real being.

day **2**

Mind is argumentative. It goes on arguing and arguing, ad infinitum. It keeps you engaged but it never gives you any conclusion. It is inconclusive – that is its nature. That's why philosophy has not been able to give a single conclusion to humanity. It has been an utterly futile exercise, and for thousands of years, thousands of the most brilliant people have remained engaged in that stupid work.

The mind argues but never reaches any conclusion; the heart argues never and knows the conclusion. This is how it is, this is one of the mysteries of life. The mind is very noisy but all the noise is useless; the heart is silent but delivers the goods.

Move from the head to the heart, from argument to no-argument and life suddenly becomes a new phenomenon, full of significance and meaning, beauty and fragrance, full of light and love. And all these combined together is the meaning of godliness.

CONTEMPLATION BEFORE SLEEP

Thoughts are like darkness, they appear just as darkness appears. It looks so real, but just bring the light in and it is no longer there. It is an appearance, something very illusory.

That's why you cannot do anything directly with darkness: you cannot throw it out, you cannot bring it in. Absolutely nothing can be done directly to darkness because it does not exist in the first place. It has no weight – it is just an absence of light. So when you bring the light in, because of its presence the absence disappears.

The same is true about mind: mind is the absence of meditation. The moment you enter into meditation, mind disappears just like darkness. And only then does one know that one has lived in a very illusory world. The mind is the world in which we live. The real world is far away from us. The mind is between us and the real, and it goes on distorting the real, interpreting the real, projecting itself on the real. It never allows you to see the reality, it never allows you to see even your own self. It becomes so important that you become focused on it, and the two realities, the outside and the inside, both disappear. The non-substantial becomes your whole life; it dominates you. You live through the mind, you live as the mind.

And that's the only problem. To live in something illusory is to live in vain. There will be no growth, no maturity, no richness, no understanding, no bliss, no truth, no beauty.

It is only the loving heart that can touch the heart of existence. The mind is shallow and superficial; it knows nothing of the heights and depths. The mind is idiotic, it is always mediocre. It cannot give you any insight into reality. For that your heart needs to function – and love is nothing but the humming of the heart.

Allow the heart to sing its song. Even if the mind condemns it, don't bother about the mind. The mind will condemn it, the mind will say, "This is irrational." For example when the situation suggests that you be miserable and you start singing a song, the mind will say, "This is not right, this is not how things should be, you have to be miserable – that is logical."

Let your heart sing, dance, rejoice. The dogs from the mind will go on barking, saying, "This is irrational, this is not expected, this is immoral." It will condemn all poetry inside you, it will condemn all love inside you. It will try every way to pull you out of the heart because its whole power is at risk. But don't listen to it; just go on singing, go on dancing, celebrating. And one day you will be surprised: the dogs are no longer barking, they have been left far behind.

The day it happens is the day of great benediction. Then flowers start showering on you, then the whole existence starts pouring all kinds of joys upon you. You are connected with the whole, you have become a seer. Love makes one a seer, it gives one eyes.

CONTEMPLATION BEFORE SLEEP

The complaining mind can never be religious. It is impossible for the complaining mind to be religious, because the complaining mind has not become aware of a basic reality: that existence loves you, that it takes care of you, that you are befriended by the winds, by the rain, by the sun, by the moon. Whatsoever happens...it may appear a curse to you, but it is never a curse, it is always a blessing. Maybe in the beginning it appears like a curse because our vision is very limited, our perspective is very small. We can't see the whole thing, we can't see all the implications of it. We can't see the whole series of events that will be followed by it; otherwise we will always be grateful, we will always feel blessed.

Even in death, a man who understands finds tremendous thankfulness towards existence, because for him death is a rest. For him death is not the end of life but the beginning of a far greater life than this one. This was just a rehearsal of the real life – it was not real.

The real drama starts after death – for those who understand. For those who don't understand they think the rehearsal is the real thing, and when the rehearsal ends, they cry and weep, and they cling, and they don't want to leave it.

Everything is a blessing!

day 6

Meditation simply means becoming empty of all the contents of mind: memory, imagination, thoughts, desires, expectations, projections, moods. One has to go on emptying oneself of all the content. The greatest day in life is when you cannot find anything to throw out – when there is only pure emptiness. In that emptiness you find your pure consciousness.

That emptiness is empty only so far as mind is concerned, otherwise it is overflowing, overfull. It is full of being – empty of mind but full of consciousness. So don't be afraid of the word 'empty', it is not negative. It negates only the unnecessary luggage which is of no use and which you are carrying just from old habit, which does not help but only hinders, which is just a weight, a mountainous weight.

Once it is removed you are free from all boundaries, you become as infinite as the sky. That experience is the experience of God or buddhahood or whatever word one likes. Call it dharma, call it tao, call it truth, call it nirvana – they all mean the same thing.

CONTEMPLATION BEFORE SLEEP

Man needs a pure heart to commune with existence. The heart becomes pure when the mind is no longer dominant within you. The heart remains impure while the mind dominates. The mind clings to the heart like dust clinging to a mirror. Mind is nothing but thought-dust. Each thought is just dust and nothing else. One has to clean all thoughts, then purity is attained.

Purity has nothing to do with morality. Of course, a pure heart is moral but a moral person need not be pure. A moral person is still living in the head; his morality is still a domination of the head. It does not know purity because it is not innocent; hence remember, morality does not lead to purity though the opposite is true. Purity certainly leads to morality, but first comes purity, then morality follows.

d
a
y
8

Our real being is our innermost core, it is not some-where outside. One need not go anywhere, one has simply to come back home. It is not a journey from here to there, on the contrary it is a journey from there to here. We are already there and we have to be here. We are always then and we have to be now.

So whenever your mind starts moving somewhere, bring it back here. When it starts moving to the past, to the future, bring it to the now. Remember these two words: now and here. Slowly slowly, one starts living herenow, and that is the only way we can meet existence, because it is always herenow. And we are never herenow. The moment we are also here now the meeting happens, is bound to happen.

CONTEMPLATION BEFORE SLEEP

It has been found recently that attention is one of the most important ingredients for any kind of growth, outer or inner. A child needs the mother's milk, but even more than that he needs the mother's attention. If the mother only gives him nourishment for the body and takes no other care, if the child feels neglected, ignored, his growth is stopped. He loses trust in himself, he loses confidence, he loses the very purpose of life. He starts feeling he is useless, he is not needed. To be needed is the greatest need. Without it, without its cosy atmosphere nothing can grow.

The same happens in the inner world: if we remain deserts we are at fault. We have not taken any care of it, we have never even bothered about it...and the most important thing is attention: pay more attention to your own centre. Whenever you have time close your eyes to the whole world and forget all about it. Shower your centre with all your attention, care, love, and soon you will see flowers coming up. It is a kind of gardening, a kind of farming, and it brings tremendous joy because when you come to see the flowers of consciousness you know that life has not been a wastage, that you have not missed the opportunity, that you have used it.

d a y

10

The ultimate experience of life is a paradox. It is the sound of silence. Now, logically that is absurd: either something can be sound or it can be silence – it can't be both together. But those who have known all agree that it is the sound of silence, it is the sound of one hand clapping. All those who have known agree about the paradoxical nature of the ultimate reality because it contains the polar opposites. It is night and day simultaneously, it is life and death together. Logic divides, experience unites. Logic creates opposites, experience makes you aware that there are no opposites at all, not at all. All opposites are just complementarities.

The definition of truth is that which is eternal. That which is not eternal is only a fact, not a truth. And the difference between a fact and a fiction is not much. That which is a fact may have been a fiction just a moment before and that which is a fiction right now may become a fact in the next moment.

Neither is fiction truth nor are facts truth. That's why in the East we have never bothered about history very much – because history consists of facts. The West is very fact-oriented.

CONTEMPLATION BEFORE SLEEP

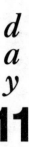

The Western mind lives in time-consciousness, the Eastern approach is towards timelessness; hence the Eastern definition of truth is that which is beyond time. So unless you go beyond time you know nothing of truth. In time you only see a film on the screen – it can be beautiful and for the moment you may become enchanted with it, but deep down you know it is just a fiction. Then the end comes and the screen is left behind and then suddenly there is the realization that for the whole time only the screen was real and the film was just a projection.

The world of facts is only a projection, the screen is the reality; but the screen is hidden behind the projection.

The screen is God and the world is just a film moving on that divine screen. How to penetrate the real – that which is and will always be and has always been? The method that we have discovered in the East is meditation. Meditation simply means dropping all fictions and facts, cleansing the mind of fictions and facts so that only the screen remains. The screen of consciousness is pure and empty, clean and white, and nothing moves on it. All movement has disappeared because all movement is in time.

Time has stopped, the clock has stopped. Suddenly you are transported into another world, the transcendental world. And that is the world of truth. To know it is to know all and to know it is to be it, because then the knower and the known are no longer separate; then the knower is the known, the seer is the seen, the observer is the observed. That is the ultimate experience which liberates, which liberates you from all the fantasies of the mind and from all the mundane facts of the world.

MONTH TWELVE

Reality is paradoxical; it contains all the polar opposites in it. Seen in the right perspective they are not thought to be opposites, they start looking like complementarities. Hence the paradox is only from the lower world of thinking.

When you yourself reach the peak of no thought, there is no paradox; you suddenly see the unity of all opposites. In the ultimate the day and night meet and merge, life and death meet and merge, summer and winter meet and merge – there is no difference....

It is very difficult to understand it intellectually because intellectually they are opposites. Intellect cannot conceive that they can happen together. But that is intellect's limitation.

When physicists for the first time discovered that the ultimate particle, the electron, which is the constituent of all matter, behaves very paradoxically, they were at a loss as to how to describe it: it behaves as a particle and also as a wave simultaneously. A particle means simply a dot. It can't be a line simultaneously. A line means many dots, a single dot is not a line. A wave is a line.

For many years there was great controversy about how to describe it, because it does not fit ordinary logic. Then they have to listen to reality. What can you do? If reality is behaving in that mad way, we have to describe it the way it is behaving, we have to put our logic aside; our logic can't be that important.

Finally they decided that it is both together. Since that day, physics has become metaphysics. Since that day physicists have started talking like mystics. They had to. And now no great physicist can say that mystics are paradoxical; now they know themselves that you cannot avoid paradox when you encounter reality.

CONTEMPLATION BEFORE SLEEP

The first step is the silence of the mind, when thoughts disappear. As you start meditating you have to begin by watching the thoughts. Just by watching, one day they disappear.

Then begins the second step: the silence of the heart. That comes by watching the feelings. It is a more subtle phenomenon, far deeper than the first, but the process is the same. If one succeeds in the first one will be able to succeed in the second too. Then the second silence is achieved. And when both these silences are there then for the first time you know that the watcher also has disappeared because there is nothing to watch. And there is nothing to know, the knower disappears. That is the ultimate silence. The first two are steps towards the ultimate, which is that silence which Buddha calls nirvana and Jesus calls the kingdom of God.

To be with a master simply means to live with someone who is awake, who is no more asleep, whose dreams are finished, whose nightmares are over. And just being in tune with the master slowly slowly wakes you up. The very energy of the master starts penetrating your being. Slowly slowly it seeps into your heart, slowly slowly it gives you a new heart, a new beat. And you cannot remain long with a master without becoming awake, because he is continuously shouting, calling you forth to wake up, calling you forth to come out of your grave.

And if you can open your eyes once, suddenly for the first time you experience the music, the song, the dance; and it goes on increasing, it goes on moving towards a crescendo, towards a height which is absolutely unimaginable to the ordinary mind. It is beyond the mind, far beyond; hence the mind cannot say anything about it. It is indescribable, indefinable. The mind simply falls short with all its logic, language, words, with all its efficiency as far as the world is concerned.

In the encounter with the beyond, the mind feels for the first time utterly impotent. The impotency of the mind releases a new energy in you. That energy I call the song, the dance, the ecstasy.... It is a kingdom. You become an emperor only when your heart is full of songs, ready to burst forth, when the energy is so much that you would like to dance and share it.

CONTEMPLATION BEFORE SLEEP

Everything is a gift. We have not earned it, we don't even deserve it. Seeing a beautiful sunset have you ever pondered over the matter: Do I deserve it? Listening to a distant call of the cuckoo have you ever thought: Do I deserve it? Or the wind passing through the pine trees or the river dancing towards the ocean and the sky full of stars – what have we done to have this beautiful universe? We have not paid for it, we are not worthy of it.

It is out of this experience – that we don't deserve it, yet it has been given to us – that religious consciousness arises, gratitude arises. One starts feeling tremendously grateful to the unknown hands, the invisible hands that have created this beautiful, this tremendously, unbelievably beautiful existence. In that gratitude one is religious – not by being a Christian or a Hindu or a Mohammedan, just by being grateful.

day **16**

The universe is vast, unbounded, and so are we because we are part of it. And the part is indivisibly one with the whole, so whatsoever is the quality of the whole, that is the quality of the part too.

Just remember a very small formula: if all the parts are finite then the total cannot be infinite. If the total is infinite then all the parts must be infinite too. And we are part of this infinite existence. We are also infinite.

Hence the Eastern seers have declared, *"Aham Brahmasmi"* – I am God. Al-Hillaj Mansoor says, *"Ana'l Haq* – I am truth."* These are tremendously important declarations. They have declared it on behalf of the whole of humanity. These are not egoistic assertions, they are simply statements of facts. And just feel it; that you are part of an infinite existence which begins nowhere, ends nowhere. You immediately feel uplifted, weightless. Your small worries and small problems drop. They become so insignificant compared to the vastness that you are. They lose all meaning, they simply become irrelevant.

CONTEMPLATION BEFORE SLEEP

Every awakened person has felt a tremendous compassion for people and he has tried his best. But something in the very experience is such that it cannot be expressed. If one wants to know it one has to experience it.

Truth can only be an experience. You are full of stars, full of flowers but absolutely incapable of transferring it to anybody. It is untransferable, it cannot be taught. But those who are alert, they can catch a glimpse of it. It cannot be taught but it can be caught.

d
a
y

18

It is impossible to express the ultimate truth. It is like a taste. If you have tasted, you know; if you have not tasted, there is no way to convey it. A man who has not tasted honey cannot be made to know what sweetness is. The man who has never seen light is incapable of understanding anything about light. The person who has known and experienced, even he finds it almost impossible to express it, because language falls very short. The experience is so vast and language is so small. The experience is so sacred and language is so mundane that there is no possibility of any bridging.

Hence the truth has been known many times and all those who have known have tried to express it but they have failed. We are grateful that they tried because out of that effort life has been enriched.

CONTEMPLATION BEFORE SLEEP

The real thing is to experience; hence my emphasis is on experience, not on belief. Don't believe what I say. Try to experience it. And unless you have experienced, resist the temptation to believe. The temptation is always there because belief is cheap. The mind says, "What is the point of investigating, inquiring, exploring? Why bother? Just believe! Buddha knows, Jesus knows, Lao Tzu knows, Zarathustra knows, so what is the point? If they are all saying that is so, it must be so." But if Zarathustra drinks, his thirst is quenched, not yours. If Zarathustra knows, he knows, not you.

Belief is death, it is a full point; you simply take it for granted. Somebody says, somebody authoritative – the Bible, the Koran, the Gita – and you simply believe the authority. To believe in any authority is to destroy your own intelligence. All authorities are destructive of intelligence.

Belief is insisted upon only by people who themselves don't know. They are afraid of inquiry, they are afraid of doubt, they are afraid of questions. They repress all questioning. They condemn all doubt. I respect it.

So I have to be just a hypothesis for you. I will give you hypotheses; then you have to go into inquiry. And I know you will find the truth, because I have found the truth through the same inquiry. I trust everybody's intelligence and everybody's intrinsic potential.

And the day you discover that you are one with the whole, you have come home. Now you feel blessed, so much so that you can bless the whole universe.

day **20**

Every person is born with a divine voice although we never hear it. It is a still, small voice. It is the voice of God. But our heads are so full of other voices – and there are a thousand and one voices – we can't hear the still small voice. And in our heads all the stations are on simultaneously. It is so noisy inside that even if God shouts you won't hear. And he never shouts, he whispers. Love always whispers because to shout is a little violent. Love knows how to wait; hence God waits. Love knows how to hope, hence God hopes. If not today, then tomorrow...some day you are going to hear. So become more and more silent, less and less noisy so that you can hear the whisper of God within you. That's the beginning of a new life, of a life that is eternal.

CONTEMPLATION BEFORE SLEEP

The most unique experience in life is that of silence; otherwise life is very noisy. Outside there is noise, inside there is noise and both together are enough to drive anybody crazy. They have driven the whole world crazy.

One has to stop the inner noise – the outer noise is beyond our control and there is no need, either, to stop it – but we can stop the inner noise. And once the inner noise is stopped and silence settles in, the outer noise is no problem at all; you can enjoy it, you can live in it without any problem. And the experience of inner silence is unique, incomparable. There is no other experience which can be of much value, because out of this experience all experiences grow. It is the foundation of the whole temple of religion.

Without silence there is no truth, no freedom, no God; with silence, suddenly things which were not there are there and things which were there are no more there – your vision has changed, your perspective has changed. Silence makes you capable of knowing the invisible, of knowing the unknowable. That's its uniqueness.

day **22**

Society has no interest in your love energy. Its whole interest is in your head, in your logical capacity, because that can be used as a commodity in the market. Society only wants you to be efficient – not meaningful, simply efficient, as efficient as a machine. But the machine has no idea of love and will never be able to have any idea of love.

As far as the head is concerned, sooner or later computers are going to replace it. What the head does computers can do in a far better way. But I don't think that any computer is ever going to fall in love. Logic is a mechanical capacity – machines can do it. The human element in you is love, but society is not interested in it, it has no use for it; hence it teaches everybody to be logical. And the more hung up in the head you become, the more you forget your heart.

God is known through the heart, truth is known through the heart. The heart is the centre from where we can take a plunge into existence. It becomes the jumping board to go into the oceanic.

Man is immortal. There is no death in fact. But how to know it from the head? There is no way. The way goes through the heart. Hence I say love is the only experience in life which makes you aware of your immortality. And once you know there is no death, your life of course will have a totally different quality to it – poetry, dance, a song, a celebration. Because there is no death one can shout "Hallelujah!"

CONTEMPLATION BEFORE SLEEP

My effort here is to help your love become greater. All the so-called religions have been trying to do just the opposite. Seeing that love creates misery they teach the renouncing of love. I also see that love creates misery, but seeing that, I teach the renouncing of limitations. Let your love become unlimited.

The so-called religious traditions and my approach begin from the same point but we move in different directions. They think it is love that is creating the trouble; I don't see that it is love that is creating the trouble. It is the limitation that you impose upon love that is creating the trouble. Renouncing love is not the solution. Renounce the limitations. Just be loving; let love be a spontaneous, natural phenomenon.

The moment you free your love from limitations you are free. The moment your love is free your very being is free because your being consists of love, your soul consists of love.

d
a
y
24

My whole effort here is to make you a little more festive, to make you just a little more joyful, to make you aware of all the gifts that the whole has given to you so that gratitude can arise in you. And out of that gratitude comes the offering of songs. Then one bows down to existence, just in simple gratefulness, and offers oneself, whatsoever one has got – a few flowers of one's being. These flowers are what I mean by songs: a little bit of creativity, whatsoever you can create.

The very feeling: "I have contributed a little bit to the beauty of the world, to the grace of existence; I have added a little more light to the dark night of the soul," and one feels fulfilled, immensely contented. Nothing more is needed, no other religion.

Creativity is religion. Creativity is prayer. But creativity can come only out of meditativeness.

CONTEMPLATION BEFORE SLEEP

There are many people who are thought to be mad simply because they are heart people and they cannot communicate with the world which has been created by the head. Their only problem is that they are in a far better space than the rest of the world. It is like a man who has eyes living with people who don't have eyes: he will be in constant difficulty. Nobody will listen to him, nobody will ever understand him; he is inevitably going to be misunderstood, on each point, on each count.

Hence very few people dare to live in the heart. They are the mystics; they have come very close – but to be close means still a little way off. One more quantum leap is needed, one more jump, and then you reach the indescribable. It is neither the body nor the mind nor the heart, and your whole language consists of words which belong either to the body or to the mind or the heart. No words exist for it.

d
a
y

26

Friendship has something spiritual about it. Love is biological; friendship is spiritual. And unless love becomes something like a friendship one suffers through it; rather than finding bliss one finds more and more misery. But the reason is not in the energy of love. The reason is that you have not been able to refine it, you have not been very artful about it. You have taken it for granted, as if this is the end. This is not the end.

Let your love become friendship; let your love become prayer. These are the two possibilities, two aspects. If you become friendly with the person you love then you can love many persons. Then your love spreads, then the circle becomes bigger and bigger. This is one aspect.

The other aspect is that when you start loving many people with no clinging and you also allow the others the same, your love starts growing another aspect – the aspect called prayer.

Prayer means loving the whole, the whole universe, becoming friendly with the trees and the rocks and the rivers and the mountains and the stars. When friendship reaches the point of prayer one is religious.

CONTEMPLATION BEFORE SLEEP

The ego has to be totally dropped. You are not to be achievers. Whatsoever you need is already given, it is already the case. All that you need is to let it grow. Your potential is there; you have to remove hindrances. You can call my thinking negative thinking against the positive thinking. The positive thinking says project your idea of who you want to be; I say existence has already made you what you are, only negate the hindrances.

That has been the most ancient teaching of the great mystics, of all the buddhas. We call the method *neti-neti*. Go on saying, "This is not me, this is not me," and go on removing everything till nothing is left to be removed. When absolute nothingness has happened, in that nothingness the lotus opens up. For the first time, when you are not, you are. And to experience this paradox is the greatest experience in life.

The really religious person is very earthly; he has to be, otherwise he won't have any roots. Hence I teach rootedness to the earth. I teach the earth, because I know that only if our roots grow into the earth will we be able to rise beyond the clouds. The flowers will come but they will come only by getting deeper and deeper roots.

So to me the mundane and the sacred are not different; they are two sides of the same coin. Hence singing and dancing and love and creativity and cheerfulness and laughter are not against the sacred. They are part, an intrinsic part of it, and not a small part – exactly half of it, and the first half. And if the first half is there the second half follows automatically. They cannot be separated. But in the past the second half became more important; not only more important, it became empty of the first half. That's how religion died. That's how God died on the earth: God became a tree without roots.

God can live again, but the only way for God to live again is to have roots in the earth – and that's what I mean by cheerfulness, song, celebration.

CONTEMPLATION BEFORE SLEEP

The lotus is very symbolic – it grows out of mud –
the most beautiful flower grows out of dirty mud.
Prayer grows out of sexuality and the soul grows out of
the body, which is just mud, and godliness grows out
of the world. On the surface it looks impossible. If you
look at mud you cannot believe that it can produce
lotuses. If you look at the lotus you cannot believe
that it can come out of dirty mud. But that's how it is,
the lowest is connected with the highest. The highest
is in the lowest and the lowest is in the highest; everything is bridged. And life is a ladder.

That's my basic teaching: nothing has to be denied,
not even the dirty mud. Everything has to be transformed into a lotus.

Man can live either in time or in eternity. Both alternatives are open because there is nothing like destiny, nothing like fate. Man is freedom: he comes without a fate. The future is open, always open, it is not determined when you are born – each act determines it. In each act is your choice, and at each step you can change the very direction of your life.

Millions of people live in time, for the simple reason that they are born in a crowd which knows nothing about eternity. Their parents have lived in time, their teachers have lived in time, their leaders have lived in time, the whole society around them lives in time, between birth and death; hence every child starts imitating. That's the way the child learns but that's also how he becomes conditioned.

Everybody has been told that time consists of three tenses – past, present and future – and that is absolutely wrong. Time consists only of past and future. The present is a penetration of eternity, the present does not belong to time; it is transcendental. To live in the present is to get out of time; to be herenow, totally herenow, is to be out of the wheel. And the miracle is that the moment you are out of time you are out of misery. Misery is a by-product of time and bliss is a by-product of eternity, of timelessness.

And one can decide to move into eternity any moment, because it is always there. In fact the past is never there but we cling to it; we cling to nonentities. And because both of our hands are clinging to nonentities we miss what is exactly in the middle of both: the present, the real, the existential.

CONTEMPLATION BEFORE SLEEP

Both our hands are full: one hand is full of the past, the other is full of the future. A part of our being is full of memories, another part is full of fantasies, dreams, projections; and between these two is the very subtle and delicate moment. It is just like a rose-flower – crushed, missed. Meditation simply means not to miss it, to get in tune with it.

Slowly slowly, empty your hands of the past and the future so you can be full of the now – and that is transformation. It opens the door to the divine.

Life is the only God. One has to live in it and one has to live intensely, passionately, not half-heartedly, not in a lukewarm way. One has to burn one's life-torch from both ends together; then even a single moment is more valuable than the whole of eternity.

Live moment to moment, but live without holding anything back. Be herenow, as if this is the last moment.

This is the way one has to live: each moment has to be the last moment, so why live life half-heartedly? You may not be able to live another moment, so put all that you have got, risk all that you have got in the moment because who knows about the other moment.

This is the way to live! And when you don't care about the result you become a lotus. The lotus has to be remembered again and again so that you can go on getting deeper and deeper into the now and here – but unattached, unclinging, untouched. No future, so that you can live totally, and no past so that you remain untouched.

Once that happens life is bliss – unbounded bliss, infinite bliss, eternal bliss.

ABOUT THE AUTHOR

Most of us live out our lives in the world of time, in memories of the past and anticipation of the future. Only rarely do we touch the timeless dimension of the present – in moments of sudden beauty, or sudden danger, in meeting with a lover or with the surprise of the unexpected. Very few people step out of the world of time and mind, its ambitions and competitiveness, and begin to live in the world of the timeless. And of those who do, only a few have attempted to share their experience. Lao Tzu, Gautam Buddha, Bodhidharma...or more recently, George Gurdjieff, Ramana Maharshi, J. Krishnamurti – they are thought by their contemporaries to be eccentrics or madmen; after their death they are called 'philosophers'. And in time they become legends – not flesh-and-blood human beings, but perhaps mythological representations of our collective wish to grow beyond the smallness and trivia, the meaninglessness of our everyday lives.

Osho is one who has discovered the door to living his life in the timeless dimension of the present – he has called himself a 'true existentialist' – and he has devoted his life to provoking others to seek this same door, to step out of the world of past and future and discover for themselves the world of eternity.

Osho was born in Kuchwada, Madhya Pradesh, India, on December 11, 1931. From his earliest childhood, his was a rebellious and independent spirit, insisting on experiencing the truth for himself rather than acquiring knowledge and beliefs given by others.

After his enlightenment at the age of twenty-one, Osho completed his academic studies and spent several years teaching philosophy at the University of Jabalpur. Meanwhile, he travelled throughout India giving talks, challenging orthodox religious leaders in public debate, questioning traditional beliefs, and meeting people from all walks of life. He read extensively, everything he could find to broaden his understanding of the belief systems and psychology of contemporary man. By the late 1960s Osho had begun to develop his unique dynamic meditation techniques. Modern man, he says, is so burdened with the outmoded traditions of the past and the anxieties of modern-day living that he must go through a deep cleansing process before he can hope to discover the thought-less, relaxed state of meditation.

In the early 1970s, the first Westerners began to hear of Osho. By 1974 a commune had been established around him in Poona, India, and the trickle of visitors from the West was soon to become a flood. In the course of his work, Osho has spoken on virtually every aspect of the development of human consciousness. He has distilled the essence of what is significant to the spiritual quest of contemporary man, based not on intellectual understanding but tested against his own existential experience.

He belongs to no tradition – "I am the beginning of a totally new religious consciousness", he says. "Please don't connect me with the past – it is not even worth remembering."

His talks to disciples and seekers from all over the world have been published in more than six hundred volumes, and translated into over thirty languages. And he says, "My message is not a doctrine, not a philosophy. My message is a certain alchemy, a science of transformation, so only those who are willing to die as they are and be born again into something so new that they cannot even imagine it right now...only those few courageous people will be ready to listen, because listening is going to be risky.

"Listening, you have taken the first step towards being reborn. So it is not a philosophy that you can just make an overcoat of and go bragging about. It is not a doctrine where you can find consolation for harassing questions. No, my message is not some verbal communication. It is far more risky. It is nothing less than death and rebirth."

Osho left his body on January 19, 1990. His huge commune in India continues to be the largest spiritual growth centre in the world attracting thousands of international visitors who come to participate in its meditation, therapy, bodywork and creative programmes, or just to experience being in a buddhafield.

OSHO COMMUNE INTERNATIONAL

The Osho Commune International in Poona, India, guided by the vision of the enlightened master Osho, might be described as a laboratory, an experiment in creating the 'New Man' – a human being who lives in harmony with himself and his environment, and who is free from all ideologies and belief systems which now divide humanity.

The Commune's Osho Multiversity offers hundreds of workshops, groups and trainings, presented by its nine different faculties:

Osho School for Centring and Zen Martial Arts
Osho School of Creative Arts
Osho International Academy of Healing Arts
Osho Meditation Academy
Osho Institute for Love and Consciousness
Osho School of Mysticism
Osho Institute of Tibetan Pulsing Healing
Osho Centre for Transformation
Osho Club Meditation: Creative Leisure

All these programmes are designed to help people to find the knack of meditation: the passive witnessing of thoughts, emotions, and actions, without judgement or identification. Unlike many traditional Eastern disciplines, meditation at Osho Commune is an inseparable part of everyday life – working, relating or just being. The result is that people do not renounce the world but bring to it a spirit of awareness and celebration, in a deep reverence for life.

The highlight of the day at the Commune is the meeting of the Osho White Robe Brotherhood. This two-hour celebration of music, dance and silence, with a discourse from Osho, is unique – a complete meditation in itself where thousands of seekers, in Osho's words, 'dissolve into a sea of consciousness'.

For Further Information;

Many of Osho's books have been translated and published in a variety of languages worldwide. For information about Osho, his meditations, books, tapes and the address of an Osho medita-tion/information centre near you, contact:

Osho International Foundation, 24 St James's Street, St James's, London SW1A 1HA
Tel: 0171 925 1900

Osho Commune International, 17 Koregaon Park, Poona 411001, India

Chidvilas Inc. P.O. 3849, Sedona, AZ 86340